WITHDRAWN

The Imaginary Jew

The Imaginary Jew

Alain Finkielkraut

Le Juif imaginaire

Translated by Kevin O'Neill

& David Suchoff

with an Introduction by

David Suchoff

University of Nebraska Press

Lincoln & London

Originally published as
Le Juif imaginaire, copyright
© Editions du Seuil, 1980

© 1994 by the University of
Nebraska Press. All rights
reserved. Manufactured in the
United States of America

Library of Congress
Cataloging in Publication Data
Finkielkraut, Alain.
[Juif imaginaire. English] The
imaginary Jew =
(Le juif imaginaire) / by Alain
Finkielkraut;
translated by Kevin O'Neill and
David Suchoff
with an introduction by David
Suchoff.
p.   cm. – (Texts and contexts;
v. 9 Includes biblio-
graphical references and index.
ISBN 0-8032-1987-3
1. Jews – France – Identity.
2. Jews –
Identity. 3. Israel and the
diaspora.
4. France – Ethnic relations.
I. Title.
II. Title: Juif imaginaire.
III. Series.
DS135.F83F56 1994
305.892'4044 – dc20
93-29382
CIP

Contents

Acknowledgments

We would like to thank Catherine Bédard for indispensable help with this translation, as well as Arthur Greenspan, Christiane Guillois, and Ilana Livni for the assistance they provided.

K.O. & D.S.

Introduction

BY DAVID SUCHOFF

Like the German critic Walter Benjamin, who died in 1940, Alain Finkielkraut has succeeded in connecting Jewish culture with the central political questions of his day. *The Imaginary Jew* is an autobiographical work of cultural criticism that reflects on the unique dilemmas of post–World War II Jewish identity and minority culture. Born in France in 1949, Finkielkraut grew up as the child of Holocaust survivors, an active member of the student upheavals of May 1968, and a writer on the Left. This book is an intellectual autobiography examining his turn from leftist radicalism to a confrontation with his Jewishness, and the problems of defining Jewish identity in a postmodern age.[1]

As the author of eleven books, however, Finkielkraut is arguably one of Europe's preeminent intellectuals, with a recognition that Benjamin never achieved during his life. He is a major commentator on European affairs as a columnist in *Le Nouvel Observateur* and now as the editor of the journal *Le Messager Européen,* which he cofounded with Milan Kundera, Philip Roth and others in 1988, as the Cold War political framework began to dissolve. What allies him with Benjamin are a concern with memory as a cultural category, and a lyrical and sometimes nostalgic style with a penetrating edge and paradoxical explosiveness that belie a kind of cultural conservatism. Memory, to be sure, is the crucial responsibility of the public intellectual for Finkielkraut, an activism rooted in the history of the European Enlightenment that his later books have sought to exemplify and promote.

vii

The same emphasis on the critical and historical responsibility of intellectuals that informs *Remembering in Vain,* his
critique of the Klaus Barbie trial, and *The Undoing of Thought,*
his sharp dissent from French partisans of a Third-World-
centered politics, is present in *The Imaginary Jew.* [2] It would be
misleading, however, to compare Finkielkraut with American
opponents of multiculturalism, such as Arthur Schlesinger,
Jr., or neoconservatives such as Allan Bloom. Memory is not
Finkielkraut's call to return to the cultural monuments of the
past, and his work is anything but an argument for minorities
to return to liberalism. It is instead a way of calling the sanctity
of constructions of the past into question, by confronting the
monumental use of history as ideological self-legitimation.
Finkielkraut challenges the false totalization behind arguments against Enlightenment universalism, charging that
they homogenize cultural difference in the name of promot-
ing it, and patronize third world cultures by ruling out their
access to universal rights. [3] The roots of this challenge are to be
found in *The Imaginary Jew*'s emphasis on cultural memory as
the memory of loss, rather than as the ideological foundation
of an ethnic essentialism. This position is in fact closer to arguments for a renewal of the public sphere, launched in Germany by Jurgen Habermas and in America by Richard Rorty,
or for a new "civic culture" that remains multicultural, in the
phrase of Henry Louis Gates, Jr. [4] Far from a neoconservative,
Finkielkraut has published a critique of the Reagan revolution, and makes a case for the public engagement of intellectuals that resembles those of his German and American counterparts in intensity if not in scope. [5]

What makes *The Imaginary Jew* a unique book, however, is
the abyss that stands at the center of its autobiographical and
critical reflections. Behind the imaginary states of post–World
War II Jewish identity for Finkielkraut is the Holocaust, the
event that, despite its determining status, "has no heirs." An

absence haunts the rhetoric of postwar Jewish identity, Fin-kielkraut suggests, as imaginary identifications with the Left, Jewish history and contemporary Israel create inflated but attenuated forms of the post-Holocaust Jewish self. Like Benjamin, whose commitment to progress was always haunted by an awareness of historical catastrophe, Finkielkraut looks to the past, where memory offers a counterweight to the conformity that threatens to erase the complexity and historical depth of Jewish identity.

The Imaginary Jew is therefore frank in facing the self-contradictions of contemporary Jewish culture. Baby-boom Jews, Finkielkraut argues, grew up identifying with the persecution of the Holocaust while knowing little or nothing of Jewish culture. The failure of a centered sense of Jewish identity to cohere is followed out in a stunning series of analyses, touching on subjects as diverse as the Portnoy figure, Judaism as a properly national concept and an essence beyond national and class definition, Marx and the Jewish Question, Israel and the Diaspora, television and politics, and the re-emergence of anti-Semitism that was already apparent in 1980. Such "imaginary" cultural constructions of Jewish identity are then set against the impossible task of remembering the Yiddish civilization of Eastern Europe that was all but destroyed in the Holocaust. Finkielkraut's project is thus both critical and redemptive: to shatter the illusory plenitude of postwar Jewish postures while redeeming the richness of Jewish heritage from the triviality of a media-saturated age.

These paradoxes of Jewish culture speak to the predicament of minority identity per se. For at its most general, *The Imaginary Jew* is concerned with the problem of how ethnic minorities are represented – to themselves and to the dominant culture – in the contemporary political world. Comparisons can be drawn, for instance, between Finkielkraut's work and *Hunger of Memory: The Education of Richard Rodriguez*

(1981) autobiographic reflections of a contemporary Mexican-American writer that center on questions of memory and ethnic identity in postmodern society. Finkielkraut's discussion of the changing currency of the term *Israelite* as a designation for the Jews of France will also remind American readers of the similar issues raised by the changing primacy of the terms *Negro, black,* and *African-American* in American culture. Issues such as "passing," of sustaining a separate culture and history while attaining social inclusion, and of self-hatred within ethnic communities are central concerns for Finkielkraut, as they were in different ways for Malcolm X and such cultural Zionists as Ahad Ha'am. The new ethnic criticism in America has something to learn from *The Imaginary Jew*'s commitment to the ethnic past, but also from its skepticism about the dominant forms of minority politics, which Finkielkraut also questioned in *The Undoing of Thought*. While considering the Holocaust as an event that has shaped twentieth-century conceptions of majority and minority culture – a role similar to the one played by anti-Semitism in Adorno and Horkheimer's *The Dialectic of Enlightenment* – Finkielkraut's paradoxical commitment to ethnicity is one that questions the possibility of cultural memory itself.

Because Finkielkraut's own political roots are in European Marxism, *The Imaginary Jew*'s ire toward the failings of the Left is unflinching; in particular, its inability and unwillingness to address the Jewish question are painted in glaring colors. Yet Finkielkraut's criticisms of Marxism and the post-'68 Left in France are born of attachment, and his emphasis on the autonomy of the Jewish question as a historical phenomenon makes him a different kind of thinker altogether from American Jewish intellectuals who took a more conservative anti-Stalinist turn. New York intellectuals such as Lionel Trilling and Daniel Bell became the first prominent generation of Jewish-American intellectuals by rejecting Marxism and paying the full price of assimilation.[6] Finkielkraut, by contrast, sought a concrete and public form of Jewish identity as an intellectual and post-Shoah Jew. The new politics of the 1960s seemed to offer the answer, in its declaration that the "private" was "political," but Finkielkraut, as his autobiographic reflections show us, ended up desiring a more concretely and public Jewish self than the politics of the Left could permit. The moving power of *The Imaginary Jew*'s quest for Jewish identity derives from this willingness to assert a cultural Jewishness that exists between two political stools. Faced with the liberal humanism that required a suppression of ethnic identity, and a Left that denied the specificity of Jewish cultural and national concerns, Finkielkraut rejects both alternatives, and remains committed to restoring complexity and depth to the cultural and political choices of Jewish life.

The French point of departure for *The Imaginary Jew*, however, is Jean-Paul Sartre's *Reflections on the Jewish Question*. The generational difference between Jews growing up in the postwar era and their predecessors in the heroic, antifascist struggle is crucial to Finkielkraut's critique, and to the unstated definition of postmodernism that his book contests. Sartre's existentialism, he implies, still knew a firm distinction between inauthentic culture and the self. The generation that fought fascism knew history firsthand and could assume its condition and escape definition by the Other, and thus become authentic Jews. For Finkielkraut as participant of May '68, however, no such self-affirmation was possible. Sartre's distinction between the authentic and inauthentic self was no longer valid for a postmodern generation in which image and personal identity had become one. The longing for "history" and politics that preoccupied the sixties and their aftermath, his introductory chapters argue, created postures, not politics. For while the culture of May '68 may have been paradigmatically postmodern in its fusion of simulacrum with reality,

it was for Finkielkraut a post-Holocaust culture in its amnesiac mode: Jews became the elevated symbols of all who were
oppressed, while concrete forms of Jewish culture and their
political predicaments in history were forgotten. Images of
the Jew proliferated, while collective memory and its critical
force were lost.

Finkielkraut's turn to remembrance, moreover, now seems
uncannily prescient concerning the politics of memory in contemporary culture. Recent controversies that have inaugurated the post–Cold War era in Europe and America have
made remembrance a crucial issue. President Reagan's decision in 1985 to visit the West German cemetery at Bitburg
where ss troops were buried unleashed a storm of protest and
finally a high level of political and cultural reflection on what
the significance of remembering the Holocaust ought to be.[7]
A few years later, the Historikerstreit, or Historians' Debate
in West Germany centered on the question of how the Holocaust should be placed in German history.[8] Both events em-
phasized a point that Finkielkraut had already made powerfully at the beginning of the 1980s in *The Imaginary Jew*: that
memories may be personal, but what is remembered is above
all else a political question. In retrospect, Finkielkraut's insis-
tence that the Holocaust was an irredeemable break, a loss
that must nonetheless be remembered, stands as an inaugural
and crucial statement in the rethinking of the past that accompanies any major historical shift. The image of the past, as
Walter Benjamin wrote, "flashes up" at crucial historical moments, and when that past is not "recognized by the present as
one of its concerns" at those junctures, it threatens to disappear irretrievably.[9]

Prompting Finkielkraut's self-criticism in *The Imaginary
Jew* is a need to preserve the memory of the Holocaust and the
Jewish culture it sought to eradicate not only against the
forces of cultural repression but, worse yet, against their re-

production in trivializing, narcissistic representations. That project took fuller shape in his subsequent book. The translation of the French title is "The Future of a Negation: Reflection on the Question of Genocide" (1982), and in that work he took on Holocaust revisionism as a cultural symptom and was unabashedly critical of support it was lent by the Left.[10] The most moving pages of that book evoke the memory of Polish Jewry, recalling similar sections in *The Imaginary Jew* that discuss the plight of parents who, as survivors, unwittingly silenced the subject while attempting to protect their children and start life afresh. Finkielkraut makes a powerful argument for the significance of such memories and their recovery. A similar emphasis on memory has emerged in recent years in forms ranging from the Video Archives for Holocaust Testimonies at Yale University to Claude Lanzman's masterpiece, *Shoah,* to work by literary critics such as Eric Santner and historians including Saul Friedlander, Dominic LaCapra, and Yosef Yerushalmi.[11] What *The Imaginary Jew* shares with these projects is an insistence that problems of Jewish memory retain a universal significance. The difficulty of representing the Holocaust, writing its history, and preserving the memory of the Shoah, as these historians and critics have shown, is intimately connected with the crisis of representation in poststructuralist approaches to history and language, and transcends the bounds of strictly Jewish concerns.

Such, in fact, was the definition of European culture that Finkielkraut gave in his acceptance speech delivered upon reception of the Prix Européen de l'Essai Charles Veillon in 1984. "Culture," Finkielkraut declared, "and perhaps even European culture," was to be understood as that which expresses part of the "life of a people, group, or collectivity but which escapes the limits of collective being."[12] Unqualified universalism of this kind is now out of fashion for good reason, as *The Imaginary Jew* makes clear in its analysis of assimilation. Universal values such as the path toward Jewish integration and emancipation lead to Jewish self-suppression, prejudice against Yiddish culture and cultural servility toward the very authorities who acquiesced in the destruction of the Jews. Finkielkraut nonetheless questions the contemporary Jewish consensus against assimilation. The flaunting of Jewish difference in post-Holocaust France, he suggests, enacts a suppression all its own by forgetting the culture of Yiddishkeit. Neither the assimilationist universalism of the past nor the hollow gestures of difference that characterized postwar Jewish youth are therefore enough. Instead, Finkielkraut argues for a confrontation with absence: not a Sartrean facing up to death that produces personal authenticity, but a facing up to the hollowness of post-Holocaust Jewish identity leading to a commitment to the value of the past. *The Imaginary Jew* is a book that begins the work of memory on which Finkielkraut's later hopes for a liberal democratic yet ethnically diverse Europe are built.

This is thus a book that defies the categories that have shaped the discussion of Jewish identity in the post-Holocaust world. Where fierce debates have raged between those who argue the centrality of Israel to Jewish consciousness and those who defend the Diaspora, Finkielkraut is a moving partisan for the not-so-lost civilization of Yiddishkeit. Yet when ideological anti-Zionism strikes its roots in European anti-Semitism, Finkielkraut mounts an important protest and stands up for Israel, all the while reminding his reader of the variety of pre–World War II Jewish culture produced by the socialist Bund, or Rosa Luxemburg, despite their failures. Throughout, Finkielkraut's tone is both harsh and affectionate, admonishing postwar Jews to have a "bit more memory" and to keep the links between personal feeling and ethical commitment of the Jewish tradition intact. *The Imaginary Jew* thus imagines a Jewish politics that is anti-assimilationist but committed to the Enlightenment, supportive of Israel while it argues for the Diaspora, and a proponent of ethnic particularism rooted in history, yet that aspires to remain in critical tension with universal ideals.

This contradictory model of ethnicity gives Finkielkraut a position that is pan-European, universalist, yet supportive of nationalist claims to independence in the former Yugoslavia and elsewhere. It is a stand evident in Finkielkraut's continuing support for democratic nationalism in Europe, which has also found expression in his strident opposition to the cultural homogenization represented by the opening of Euro Disneyland in the outskirts of Paris.[13] Echoes of this argument for ethnic and regional autonomy are to be found in *The Imaginary Jew*. There can be no uncritical return to the hopes of nineteenth-century Jewish liberals for a universal culture, especially with American commodity culture looming as its postmodern form. Yet despite its passionate support for preserving Jewish culture, *The Imaginary Jew* goes to great length to make us mistrust the seductive subjectivity of its author's reflective, personal mode. More than a love of contradiction is involved: the personal voice for Finkielkraut seeks a memory that is collectively and historically specific to Jewish culture and history, yet hostile to the ideological conformity that definitions of ethnic identity can enforce.

Regardless of Finkielkraut's constant warnings against narcissistic indulgence in the Holocaust, the book's most unforgettable sections remind the contemporary Jewish audience that Jewish culture in the twentieth century rests on a loss felt in large things and small. Still, Finkielkraut's partisanship for Yiddish culture differs radically from *Fiddler on the Roof* sentimentality that often shrouds recollections of pre-Holocaust Jewish life. *The Imaginary Jew* counters the sentimental flattening-out of shtetl and urban life in Eastern Europe by evoking the Yiddishists, socialists, secular and indifferent Jews who gave the civilization its depth. Finkielkraut is clear-eyed and critical, moreover, of the prejudice Western European Jews themselves showed toward their less "cultured" core-ligionists from the East as they fled Russian pogroms. The paradox he emphasizes is sharp: Memory can eradicate the past just as surely as forgetting it, if the picture it draws is always a pleasant one. Media spectacles such as the television series *Holocaust,* he points out, pour out sympathy for the archaic Jews of the East while failing to provide any concrete sense of their culture. The sympathetic and archaic image, he suggests, establishes a teleology of extinction already under way as the Final Solution began its work, thus relativizing the unprecedented innovation of the Nazi crime. The key to the longing for the past in Finkielkraut is not nostalgia, but negation – the continuous sense that every act of memory, like the silence of his parents about Yiddish culture, hides a deeper and more painful truth.

Most poignantly, however, *The Imaginary Jew* describes the self-contradiction of contemporary Jewish identity as a family affair. In many ways, Finkielkraut's book can be read as an updated version of Kafka's *Letter to His Father,* sharing its longing for the parents' culture and resistance to assimilation and accommodation as facts of Jewish life. Instead of the attenuated Judaism Kafka received from his parents, Finkielkraut argues that the post-Holocaust effect was to hand down an empty and simultaneously inflated sense of what Jewish identity might mean. Being a proud Jew became important, in other words, precisely when the Holocaust robbed European Jewish culture of its content. Many parents, hoping to forget the horrors they underwent, silenced the very Yiddish culture and sense of connectedness that their children longed to possess. The generation that survived the Holocaust could identify with Israel as a new image for the Jew. But children could feel Jewish only by rebelling against their own tradition. Criticizing an Israel that was increasingly identified with the West made them feel like *Jews,* entitled to the yellow star of ostracism they had been denied by date of birth. Both stances, Finkielkraut suggests, were imaginary in their avoidance of a negation that was difficult to face: the eradication of Diaspora Jewishness as an integral Jewish culture.

Such skepticism, *The Imaginary Jew* suggests, is one of the enabling cultural challenges of our time. For Finkielkraut can be seen as one of the first intellectual figures to argue that what we roughly call postmodernity – with its proliferation of images, identities without substance, and textuality-centered culture – is in fact the post-Holocaust era. The fundamental shift in twentieth-century conceptions of language and individuality from "centered" to "decentered" conceptions bears a profound analogy to Finkielkraut's description of the post-Holocaust Jewish self.[14] Informing *The Imaginary Jew*'s account of personal and political struggle is the underlying sense that an absent presence – the Holocaust as ruptural yet unspoken force – stands behind the proliferating images and discourses of postwar cultural thought. It was Theodor Adorno who argued that Auschwitz was the central event of our age; Shoshana Felman, Claude Lanzmann and others have more recently suggested that the need and simultaneous impossibility of narrating the Holocaust remain the informing and unattended event of contemporary culture.[15] *The Imaginary Jew* gives its readers something like the autobiographic experience of such recognitions, and a sense of the Holocaust's challenge to Finkielkraut's certainties as a postwar Jewish intellectual and to the certainties of postwar culture as a whole.

The Imaginary Jew's concluding essay, "Plea for the Indeterminable," to be sure, is a kind of program for a pluralistic Jewish identity. The many strains of Jewish culture and history, he argues, defy narrow ideological, religious, national or linguistic definition, and allow Jewish culture, as the German-

Jewish philosopher Franz Rosenzweig hoped, to connect itself in moral relevance with cultures beyond its bounds. That programmatic plea, however, is always an intimate one in this book – memory is the admonitory sentinel that stands at its political gates. Finkielkraut confesses in his own conclusion that the "imaginary" Jewish outsider he had become began to fail him not as a result of political change or the disappointments of Marxism. The reflections that make up this book began when he realized his parents would one day die and, with them, the knowledge of prewar Jewish civilization he would never be able to possess. *The Imaginary Jew* is a work that explains much about Finkielkraut's stature and positions as a contemporary cultural critic. Yet it is also a profoundly personal book. The shapes of contemporary Jewish identity Finkielkraut sketches are contradictory, unsettling, but also familiar in a way that recalls what is finally Walter Benjamin's most striking image of the cultural critic: Moving forward through catastrophe, Finkielkraut too progresses in backward fashion, with his face turned toward the past.

PART ONE
The Romance of the Yellow Star

1

The Protagonist
Introduced

If I were to write my autobiography, I would call it "The Story of an Adjective." – Isaac Babel

The typical scene of humiliation is the courtyard of a parish or grammar school. In the background there sounds the continuous and confusing din of children shrieking, running, and jostling one another in order to release, in the few minutes allotted to recess, energies pent up during those all-too-long hours of class. Some, alone or still, wait silently to return to their room. Others talk excitedly. A boisterous group has made a soccer ball from knotted rags. As usual, two trees in the courtyard mark one goal while directly opposite several book bags heaped into two piles mark the other. Five against five, with an alternating goalie: the match begins under the watch of few but feverish fans. Because of the school schedule, the game must be played in bits and pieces – continued at the next break, it will be finished at lunch. The boys are charged up and unsparing. They are, as they say on television, physically into the game. And since there is no referee, every close call provokes endless bickering between the two teams. The match is constantly interrupted until, inevitably, the point is reached when the disputes turn into a fight. Two players, enraged, threaten and insult one another. With his store of slurs exhausted, one of them shouts: "Go to hell, you dirty Jew!"

The other, dumbstruck, at first looks about in search of help. Naturally he expects general indignation. But no one seems to react to the force of the remark. As if this were only one insult among others – an outrageous epithet, to be sure, but hardly more so than the "asshole" or "scum" the two opponents have already hurled at one another during the game. Eyes welling with tears, the "dirty Jew" confronts his classmate, whom, despite his indignation, he has not yet had time to hate. He attacks with his fists but the blows are weak, a response to the claims of conscience. A crowd of kids has formed, egging on the fight, chanting, "Blood! Blood!" But the scuffle is cut short. The name-caller wants to get back to the game, for soon the bell will sound, and the victim is so hard pressed to turn his embarrassment into vengeance that he gives up the fight and quits the match, secretly hoping that the others will call him back. But the gesture has no effect. His departure is met with indifference, regarded as whim or momentary sulking. And the game goes on.

Alone in his corner, the dazed child contemplates his wound. No longer an equal among equals, he has been given the plainest proof that he is a member of a despised tribe. Jew. His entire life and more will not tame the violence of this revelation.

Of course the term isn't entirely unknown to him: he attended a Bar Mitzvah a year before, which, incidentally, bored him to death, and his parents have already told him of anti-Semitism and its history of persecutions. His familiarity with the word *Jew* before the incident was vague – less, far less than a full-fledged identity, and, if anything, just the purely negative impression of being neither Catholic nor Protestant. Nothing, finally, that might prepare him for the worst, that is to say, for exclusion. Now, suddenly, in the guise of today's

4

banal altercation, this child like any other has been informed that he is not like others; for the first time he feels within himself the raging impotence of the pariah. For the first time he is excluded from the common circle because he is Jewish, disdained by peers and provided by them with a self-image that is both disgusting and bizarre. He is isolated, cut off, unable to find in his bodily features or inner being the cause of this banishment. The insult is an act of baptism: the persuasion of which he is still unsure has become his truth and his name. He was nothing but a succession of moods before, or perhaps he was defined by his class ranking – but on this day he is bestowed with an eternal identity that he can neither reject nor recast.

The match has started up again, the circle has closed without him, he is exiled from the world by an injustice that he is powerless to oppose. But of course the ostracism will not last. After the several days of solitude demanded by his sense of honor, he will return to the circle. The gang will welcome him as if nothing has happened, once again he will know glory as one of the great dribblers, and if his team ever wins, savor the sweet pleasures of communion. But the damage has been done to his innocence and cannot be repaired; one does not forget such an event. In the midst of the idyll, of such moments of bonding, he will have the uneasy feeling that a new expulsion is at hand. I am Jewish: this consciousness of a hidden uniqueness, of an invisible and ineffaceable difference will condition each move that he makes. Later, perhaps, he will choose to "pass," and invest all the skill at his disposal in blatantly dissimulating his identity to flee the Semitic malaise. Perhaps he will transform this cutting term – *Jew* – into an intransigent, determined, harsh word, one of self-affirmation and defiance. Perhaps he will search the treasure of Jewish wisdom for something to turn the infamous reproach that has been affixed to him, one day at recess, into a mark of value and worth. Whatever his future decisions might be, he will never recover from this trauma.

But you already know this episode. A multitude of writers have recited it to you in innumerable versions. It is the uplifting story of pathos in which a child is snatched from innocence and born into Judaism, the story of an injury, or better, a curse. I myself would like to address and meditate upon the opposite case: the case of a child, an adolescent who is not only proud but happy to be Jewish and who came to question, bit by bit, if there were not some bad faith in living jubilantly as an exception and an exile. Certainly a coming to moral consciousness is at work here as well, but a slow, imperceptible one far from the theatrical kind. The adventure I speak of cannot be grasped in narrative: it was a drama without a fateful event, without a discernible rupture between before and after. It was a lengthy awakening that never took the form of a fall or a "rebirth." No mythic moment can capture the progressive malaise that taught me to give up my cozy domicile in the Jewish condition.

This is not to say that I have been miraculously preserved from anti-Semitism. I too have my collection of outrages, which I still exhibit on special occasions. Untouched by time, in the back of my mind are all sorts of insults I've managed to receive – from the catechism student, dripping with a bit too much zeal, who wanted to drag me to church in order to restore me to the straight and narrow, and perhaps, who knows, to receive congratulations from the chaplain for this superb feat of conversion, to a friend on vacation, a nice guy, cool and all that, who at a turn in the conversation remarked with peremptory calmness that six million Jews killed during the war had not been enough . . . Like any Jewish child I have known the straightforward racism of camp or gym classes. It was not in books that I first encountered the word *kike,* and yet it would call for either complacency or blindness on my part to

have my story begin with the tragedy of a schoolboy, surrounded by proof of his sameness, suddenly finding himself
completely different. Convinced, on the contrary, that fate
had made me a completely different individual, unconsciously
I realized that I was almost the same, and that *I did not deserve*
the sense of historical preeminence that had inebriated my adolescence. The paradise from which I have been expelled is not
one of concord, harmony and homogeneity but a region inaccessible to common mortals, an aristocratic Eden where dissi-
dence held pride of place and which only outlaws and rebels
might enter.

Think of it then: the Judaism I had received was the most
beautiful present a post-genocidal child could imagine. I in-
herited a suffering to which I had not been subjected, for
without having to endure oppression, the identity of the victim was mine. I could savor an exceptional destiny while remaining completely at ease. Without exposure to real danger,
I had heroic stature: to be Jewish was enough to escape the an-
onymity of an identity indistinguishable from others and the
dullness of an uneventful life. I was not immune to depression, of course, but I possessed a considerable advantage over
the other children of my generation: the power to dramatize
my biography. Only in an illusory sense were we cast together
into the same misty and monotonous stretch of time; between
their mediocrity and mine was an uncrossable barrier. They
knew the torpor of untroubled waters; the tranquility I lived
was always contradicted from within by the inherent precar-
iousness of my condition. Judaism for me was a way of redeeming the quotidian. My life insignificant? The banality of
my gestures was but an illusion: a docile student, a homebody,
but within I was a nomad, a wandering Jew. A yellow-bellied
petit bourgeois, in my dreams I was ready to strike back in violence against the fury of the pogroms. I projected the more
profound truth of exile onto my sedentary existence; in every

moment of peaceful times I sensed the coming thunder of the apocalypse. In short, I was safe, but I had a remedy for the anguish that arises from excessive security: I was Jewish. The calvary of my people gave my life a prestige and a beauty that I would have been unable to discover in its own unfolding. I resolved to search my origins for the memorable stories I was denied by the uninterrupted flow of the wise and studious existence I led.

No more than the next person was I spared the metaphysical assaults of the question "Who am I?" Psychologically indecisive, lacking any clearly distinguishing personal traits, a pronounced tendency to imitate, with multiple and contradictory role models, none of which had enough authority to ensure it would prevail, prey to a constant worry of being nothing – I was well aware of the self-indulgent torments of a sheltered life. But at the moment of greatest crisis, when conscious certainty of my identity hung in the balance, I mobilized this magical fact: I am a Jew, that is, interesting, mysterious, unique; I have a history and countenance molded by twenty centuries of suffering. I can easily, when feeling low, curse my absence of personality, my inconsistencies and my hesitations – there is in me a deeper truth than that of character. Jew: in the worst moments of doubt this simple word kept me afloat. I was singled out, individualized: I escaped the vertiginous feeling of a dissolving self.

Me against them, faced off against Others. This is the romance and narrative in which I have spent the greater part of my life. Raised by indefeasible decree above the crowd and common destiny, set apart from peers without their becoming aware, I was the outsider, skinned alive, the survivor, and I couldn't savor the image enough.

Let those unfortunate members of the overwhelming majority, let those pathetic, average people, learn the ways of revolt. Me, I had been born recalcitrant. Just as they say of the

8

son of a good family that he is well-born – not a blue blood but red-blooded – I had a rebellious pedigree. Without effort I was freed from the charge of prejudice, since for society I was its scandalous emblem. I was, if I might put it this way, offered a dispensation from every stupidity, exempted from any conformity by a privilege called Judaism. With it understood once and for all that the world was divided into torturers and victims, I belonged to the camp of the oppressed. I had no need of consciousness raising or of a dose of reality: from Spartacus to Black Power, an instinctive and unconditional solidarity united me with all the earth's damned. Was I not myself the living reproach that suffering humanity aimed at its executioners? From Judaism I drew neither religion nor a way of life, but the certainty of superior sensitivity.

Since I was an admirer of Sartre at the time, with what gluttonous pleasure did I avail myself of the vocabulary he bestowed upon my existence. This inspired philosopher, without hesitation I put him at my service and made him my tailor, and the outfit he created for me was luxurious, a true mantle of enlightenment . . . His language carried my sense of conviction all the better, transforming my complacent sense of well-being into courage and confidence. With unimpeachable rigor he told me that I was an *authentic* Jew, that I *assumed* my condition and that courage, even heroism were required for me to claim so loudly and so strongly my ties to a people in disgrace. The preferred terms of Sartre literally intoxicated me: in their sublime style I read an inscription of my life, and my pronouncements of fidelity appeared to me as so many noble deeds. Who could have resisted such a subtly persuasive form of flattery? The enchantment of Sartre's prose filled the gap between what I imagined myself to be and the existence I actually led. I was a nice Jewish boy, indulging myself in nomadic fantasies and a revolt without risk, subject to none of their malaise. Sartre gave me a way to feel worthwhile, whispered to me words of self-celebration. Without having earned it, I assumed possession of an extraordinary history and had the right to find it difficult to boot! Under the spell of my own image, I immersed myself in a dream to which *Reflections on the Jewish Question* gave the harsh and virile cast of reality: the authority on authenticity served as a caution to my blusters, the master at puncturing ploys of bad faith offered, for a good while, validation of my most infatuated and histrionic airs.[1] The expert had given his verdict: my megalomania proved itself well-founded, for my gestures were in fact actions and my acting-out a form of commitment.

It's true, from as far back as I can remember, Jewishness has never been a bother or a burden for me. It was not with lowered voice or frightened or fearful murmur that I used to confess my origins. Where others made discrete mention of their ancestry (vaguely, as if it were an obscure fault, a biological blemish or social handicap), I would broadcast my own, I was its herald. Some in my circle marveled at such nerve. Instead of cowering like a cornered cat, following what they believed to be an age-old rabbinic reflex, I did an about-face and provoked the enemy. Big deal! Such a hero! Has there ever been a gentleman who blushed in shame at his coat of arms? How could I ever be embarrassed again by this Judaism, an honor, to my mind, a thousand times more worthy than a title of nobility? I was much too proud of my genealogy to think for a minute of hiding it. What was taken for my valor was, when all is said and done, simply the result of my immodesty.

Except for my parents and two or three uncles and aunts, I have no family. And it was by miracle alone that these few close relatives survived the general massacre of Polish Jews. I lived (and still live) surrounded by the vanished, whose disappearance increased my worth without managing to make me suffer. The interminable list of all these dead I've never known created my nobility. No doubt, when my parents recounted their nightmare journey through five years of war, and related what had become of their group, I was more than moved. I would cry in anguish and in anger. But I did so in vain, for the sorrow born of their story vanished with it, just as we forget the plot once the book is closed. The terror left no traces. Beyond the representation made me, its existence could not be sustained. It slipped with all its baggage into the nothingness that had gone before. In short, despite my efforts, I didn't carry the burden of mourning my exterminated family, but I did carry its banner. I, too, would recount family stories of the final solution, and my interlocutor, seized by a mixture of stupefaction, shame and respect, would see in me something other than myself: the faces of those tortured to death. Medusalike, I petrified my public. Others had suffered and I, because I was their descendant, harvested all the moral advantage. The allotment was inescapable: for them, utter abandonment and anonymous death, and for their spokesperson, sympathy and honor. Since the actors had been annihilated, it was left to their narrator, their heir, their offspring to appropriate the reaction of their audience. At the end of the play, he alone came front-stage to bow before the applause. The effect produced wasn't intentional. I did not deliberately turn the catastrophe to the shallow ends of self-aggrandizement. I did not set out like a cynical and sordid swindler to embezzle what they possessed. But it isn't only intention that matters: while I was quite capable of assuming a sober tone and forcing myself to disappear into the story, in fact I showed off, amazed the gallery, commanded the admiration of the spectators. A part of myself had perished in Auschwitz, in a Polish forest or in the Lwów ghetto; I owed to the bond of blood this intoxicating power to confuse myself with the martyrs.

Lineage made me genocide's huckster, its witness and practically its victim. Before telling the story of my origins, I was simply an individual; afterward, there appeared an un-heard-of character like someone miraculously healed, or a ghost. With this sort of investiture, any other title seemed wretched or ridiculous to me. Hence my remarkable lack of complexes. Most children, they say, like to invent an illustrious birth. They devote their secret dreams to changing parentage, to imagining an adventurous or princely family background for themselves. What need had I of such mythologies? What great lord, what bohemian artist could rival my ancestry? No more hyperbolic world existed than the one into which I had been born. My narcissism found its sustenance on the spot, and the fiction of my family romance always unfolded at the heart of my own family.

Thus, there was no virtue in my ostentation: I forged a tragic spectacle from the tragedy of my people, and I was its hero. In short, I played at being persecuted, and did so in the mode of pantomime or the purely ceremonious gesture that I carried off without actually compromising myself. I was a swashbuckler of the concentration camps – but why accuse myself? My date of birth alone explains this propensity to bombast. I was born too close to the Holocaust to be able to keep it from view, and at the same time I was protected by all the horror of this event from a renewal of anti-Semitism, at least in its organized and violent form. In a sense, I was *overjoyed*: the war's proximity at once magnified and preserved me; it invited me to identify with the victims while giving me the all but certain assurance that I would never be one. I had all the profit but none of the risk. I could, knowing my immunity, revolt against torture and racism. History – in irony or generosity – had made me a superfluous rebel in a peaceful era. Expatriate deluxe, a deportee for the fun of it, I lived in the security of anachronism.

Does this mean that anti-Semitism is an outmoded relic, best relegated to the museum of horror and superstitions between the fear of witches, the practice of magic and devil worship? Nothing permits such optimism. And above all not what one calls the lessons of experience. Each time, in history, that anti-Jewish violence has seen a lull, we have wanted to read this fleeting break as an ineluctable decline. Finally, we'd sigh, the world was leaving the Middle Ages behind. Each time, we were mistaken. It would require a heavy dose of ignorance or presumption to certify, on the basis of today's relative tranquility, that our epoch is any different.

The future of the Jews cannot be foreseen. In this matter only provisional truths are justified. Our contemporary truth is that the Jews are rather popular in Western Europe, and that they owe this rehabilitation in large part to the barbarism of the Nazis and its trauma. If there had not been death camps, Judeophobic prejudice would remain not only widespread (as it perhaps still is) but offensive and blatant. Let us imagine that in 1939, a fit of German conscience had driven Hitler from power and reestablished democracy. The insult "dirty kike" would still be part of our daily experience. It is only taboo now because forty years ago it was carried out to the letter by the regime of the Reich. The very goal of Hitlerism was, in effect, destruction of the barrier traditionally raised between hate speech and the murderous act. The classic slogans of anti-Semitism have been so effectively transformed into reality that they have lost, in a single stroke, all ritualistic or symbolic force. Today one can no longer say "Death to the Jews," because this death has taken place. The waning of rhetorical anti-Semitism follows active measures of political anti-Semitism. Silence becomes the norm, because it is no longer possible to fashion a release or a verbal exorcism out of an effective program of annihilation. The call for murder, which, during the Dreyfus affair, was made without reference to any specific situation and constituted an end in itself, has in the meantime been burdened with history and is no longer anything but an advocacy of Auschwitz. The artistic haziness of unanchored words is over; the convenient distinction of words from acts doesn't hold in this domain; anti-Semitic opinion can scarcely be dissociated from the image of charnel houses. This is what discourages, understandably, many anti-Jewish candidates for office (though not all, and it's this minority that perseveres in hatred that is truly unbelievable). In any case, as long as genocide survives in European memory, only a small number of people will devote themselves to this activity so common before the war: the suppression of the Jews in word or dream.

Thus I lived in a veritable cocoon. Nothing to fear, my two bodyguards warded off problems and prevented unpleasant surprises: history, kind enough to exempt me from its convulsions, and my mother, seized by a devouring and protective passion for me, dedicated body and soul to my personal bliss, as if she wanted to make amends, at every moment, for the initial risk to which she had exposed me by giving birth to a Jewish child. Tradition and psychology work together here: whether one is a Jew, in our time, is more than ever determined by the mother. She's the one who overfeeds us because she has known privation and who idolizes us because she was orphaned. One does not recover from such adoration. Egocentric and infantile, the children of a "Jewish Mother" are easily recognizable. These members of the brotherhood of Portnoys could not pass unnoticed even if they wished. As adults, they have the vulnerability and the look of children who've been loved too much. What there is of the Jew in them is not, as they would like to believe, the wisdom of wandering and the sorrow of persecution, but the impotence of an overgrown baby who is pampered, adorned, cuddled and powdered until old age. Identifying characteristic: mama.

These cherubic, overnourished, pot-bellied men fancy themselves to be Isrolik, little Tom Thumb of the Ghetto, the waif of the streets. They mask their inborn softness with the outcast's courage. But the bravado is false. For these mama's boys, Jewish history is a lullaby, the song that peoples their sleep with heroic dreams and permits them vicarious experience of the horror. Cowards in life, martyred in dream – they love historical self-deception, confusing the sheltered world in which they live with the cataclysm their parents endured. Among Jews they constitute a strange but widespread category, one that has not yet found a name. They are not religious, at least most of them; in vain they cherish Jewish culture, possessing only its sorry relics. They have not performed their apprenticeship to Judaism under the gaze of the Other. Neither ethnic nor denominational definition nor the Sartrian scheme could suit them. They are unwavering Jews, but armchair Jews, since, after the Catastrophe, Judaism cannot offer them any content but suffering, and they themselves do not suffer. In order to deny this contradiction, they have chosen to pass their time in a novelistic space full of sound and fury that offers them the best role. Like fanatics of the printed word who flee, by reading, the provincial boredom in which they languish, like spectators who project their desires, their frustrations into a panting plot they will never live – spellbound, these young people live in borrowed identities. They have taken up residence in fiction. The Judaism they invoke enraptures and transports them magically to a setting in which they are exalted and sanctified. For these habitués of unreality, more numerous than one might suppose, I propose the name "imaginary Jews."

2

All German Jews?

Grandiose words should whistle like a teapot, in which water is heated, as a warning. – Elias Canetti

I remember that day in May 1968 when we heard on the radio that Daniel Cohn-Bendit had been denied permission to return to France. Thousands of people gathered spontaneously in the streets, and began to chant: "We are all German Jews!" In their disgust, the demonstrators affirmed their complete solidarity with a man whom inept authorities had elevated to symbolic status – the denial of an entry visa added glamorous distinction to his already considerable prestige. Yet for all the sincerity the demonstrators possessed, their indignation tells only half the story. The improvised march was also a festival: Jewish identity was no longer for Jews alone. The event taking place put an end to such exclusivity. Every child of the postwar era could change places with the outsider and wear the yellow star. The role of the Just now belonged to whoever wished to assume it; the crowd felt justified in proclaiming its own exceptional status, which largely explains the exuberant cheer of its members.

As a Jew, I joined my voice with the clamor, chanting the slogan in unison, but did so with mixed emotions, no doubt feeling as much irritated as thankful. I was stirred by the refusal and its unvarnished denial of due process, encouraging as it did the latent anti-Semitism of the public, but I found the protesters' generosity far too facile and flashy. It was as if, deep down, the slogan "We are all German Jews" despoiled me and sullied my treasure, as if the demonstrators, while assuring me of their complete support, had picked my pocket of my special status. "Hands off," I felt like saying. "You can't become a Jew or a dago just like that. You need certification, references. German Jews? With your French-looking faces? What gives you the right to reap the rewards? You haven't paid your dues."

Without really venturing to articulate my discomfort, I was troubled by the fact that the crowd, especially my comrades, had adorned themselves with a status too rare and distinctive for their use. I was a little bit like the bourgeois who's just been mugged and doesn't know where to turn.

It took me a while to get over this mood of resentment, but I gradually realized that the muffled anger separating me from the protesters could have been directed at myself. What right did I have to be irritated? I hadn't suffered either, nor paid my tribute of tears. In judging others to be usurpers of the Jewish condition, it was impossible not to condemn myself, and belonging to the people of Israel only made things worse. Their disguise was temporary, donned for the length of a demonstration; for me every day was a costume party. I was a Jew, and frankly, I never had to take off my disguise.

In fact, the only thing I could really hold against these ephemeral German Jews was their caricature of my own Jewishness. They were Jews, but only for the sake of the image, just as I was, just as at any given moment our entire generation might strike an anarchist, Trotskyist or Maoist pose.[1]

To each his place in history. The place history had accorded us, the posterity of the baby boom, was the ludicrous agony of growing up during the "phony peace." Our favorite pastime in an era so devoid of significance was transforming it into war or insurrection. Nothing was going on, so we fashioned the nothingness that befell us into the gaudy garb of revolution.

How many identities we assumed, one after the other! Colonized natives with Frantz Fanon, American blacks with Malcolm X and LeRoi Jones, guerrillas with Che, partisan strategists with Giap or Ho Chi Minh, we desperately strove to plug into the great revolt of the day, never realizing that what made us unique was this quest itself. For the frenzy of our search defined us far better than the fleeting content it expressed. Terrorized by our insignificance, we are the silly and complex-laden generation united by slogans, greedily claiming every uprising of the twentieth century as our own. And since, as they say, travel shapes one's youth, this rapid series of armchair journeys shaped our coming of age.

Looking back on their lives, our illustrious predecessors spoke to us of an experience each of them had shared. Sartre, Merleau-Ponty, Simone de Beauvoir or Althusser diverged, to be sure, in the political positions they took. But the trajectory of each was the same: an egotistical youth, followed by a care-free and comfortable adolescence, and finally the Popular Front and Spanish Civil War. And the war came, as if an apotheosis. History swoops down like a vulture. Individuals with no particular predilection for collective struggle, preoccupied with their personal problems, were subjected with scarcely a warning cry to what Althusser called "the terrible education of facts." These were the tales of initiation we piously gathered. Never, we vowed, would we succumb to such illusions ourselves. Once there were such petit bourgeois, suited only for a life of refinement and who, violated by politics, never recovered from the crime. Not us; we would reject the every-man-for-himself economy, set the epoch of individualism to the torch, taking our positions at the front from the start. Why fool around? Our consciousness had already been raised. With the warning of our predecessors in mind, we would not wait for History to awaken us in the middle of a nap, while refining our sensibilities or humming a tune by Charles Trénet.

No, as zealous subjects of the revolution we would report early, go on active duty before the call to arms was heard.

There was, of course, no trace of egotism in this view, none of the sins the prewar generation retrospectively imputes to itself. If, as Gorky writes, the petit bourgeois is he who likes himself best, we were the farthest thing from petit bourgeois. Our generation had so little self-regard that it was in constant need of masks; we could only bear to face ourselves unrecognizably disguised. How could anyone honestly accuse us of being selfish or egocentric? Properly speaking, we had no ego and replaced the self with a supply of glossy images, sustained by an indefatigable power of projection. Ours was a generation with a genius for mimicry. Yet it never occurred to these activists, who professed only contempt for those who lived in *forgetfulness of history,* that their own political commitments rested on a *phantasm of history* at best. Although not blind to current events, the protesters' vision of the present was always colored by the crushing, monumental weight of the fathers' past. The struggle against fascism, the International Brigades, the Resistance, the gigantic shadow of the October Revolution, the terrible clash between Trotsky and Stalin, Mao's Long March, the romance of Castro's guerrillas – the generation of 1968 had its head stuffed full of legendary tales. Proclaiming itself firmly grounded in history, even claiming the status of the historical avant-garde, this generation arrogantly ignored the fact that phantoms possessed it, and that pastiche was the governing principle of its deeds.

Though students deprived of great battles, we remained avid zealots, always on the lookout for a chance to fight. Our famous forefathers were asleep when suddenly the horrors of a world in crisis shook them from their torpor. And us? Why we were a generation of insomniacs, striving to live with our eyes open lest we be caught snoring on the job. The result: instead of surrendering to sleep, we succumbed to our own hallucinations. An entire epoch made symbolic identification practically its only way of relating to the world.

And where did it come from, this arrogant style we displayed from time to time? Of course, we weren't born yesterday. They couldn't pull the wool over our eyes. We knew it all: that every action was political, from the confrontation of States to the most intimate event; that Capital operated through mystification and sought to insinuate itself in our consciousnesses; that a merciless combat was under way between the bourgeoisie and the working class, and that not taking part was still to choose a side. Take a look at our faces back then, furrowed by experience that was not our own. Though historical novices, we had the self-possession of those who have passed the test of fire, gone through initiation rites. We were that monstrosity: snide children.

Overwhelmed by the immense memory of all we had not lived, we aped everything, even the lucidity of our masters. Our frantic masquerade sought to appease bad conscience, to deny the gap between our enjoyment of baby-boom comforts and the momentous, terrifying events of the recent past. Through such acts of fictive intensity, we exorcised the vapidity of our lives. Day-to-day experience, for us, was prose, and politics was poetry. It was inconceivable that we might live in prose. To be militant was to change our genre: our existence, unseen and unknown, was moving on to occupy a higher, superior realm. All German Jews? Come on: we were all imaginary Jews.

> Dream is reality, the students wrote on the wall, but it seems that the opposite was true: their reality (the barricades, the overturned cars, the red flags) was a dream."[2]

The militant, so crucial a character in the years '68–'73, has no place in the coming decade. He has perished in the flames of a double accusation. With morality having become a property of Desire rather than Virtue, we could see nothing but self-censorship or inhibition in his absolute devotion to the party, the group or the Cause. More deeply, we discovered that the Cause itself, beneath its apparent generosity, contained the seeds of the most implacable tyranny. The militant was to be condemned for his *puritan* mentality and *totalitarian* inclination, in the name of libido and liberty. Only a single trait of the militant has been retained: his sense of theater, his taste for big productions. Though the repressive sublimations of the partisan have disappeared, we have carefully avoided disturbing its essence – theatricality. *Utopia* is a devalued term, and communism a concept in disrepute, but for all that, the stage is still full. The show must go on. Ladies and Gentlemen, welcome to the grand era of the dissident. "From comrade to dissident," so one could title the bittersweet metamorphoses we underwent. How many memberships, hesitations and withdrawals took place between these two poses! Yet still the impression remains that nothing has really changed; the actors have simply changed garb.

Resistance to the gulag, today's buzzword, means just about the opposite of what the term *revolution* once meant, but the attraction of each is the same. Slogans aren't preferred for their content: their magnificence seduces. Such words are mirrors that we pretend are categories of analysis: we love to see ourselves reflected in them and to gaze at the beautiful image they produce. Has the hour of disillusionment come? Perhaps, but the sobered balance sheet of the era bathes in the same unreal aura as the delirium it succeeds. We agonize over conscience just as we once lived out our grand lyrical fancies: using other peoples, on the backs of the true actors. The facts don't matter; it's a different kind of game. France is not a totalitarian country? We'll usurp the condition of dissident all the same, casually, eagerly, just as we took possession of the revolutionary's condition: in order to be someone, and to satisfy our epic ambitions. In the long list of characters with whom our generation has identified, the dissident follows, without a hitch, the maquisard or the guerrilla.

And don't forget that we were born at the same time as television. We grew up with the media age; from tender youth, the world as audiovisual spectacle has been our daily fare. Our coming of age was doubly transfixed, both by the century's grand struggles and by the incessant broadcast of images across the small screen. Encouraged to become voyeurs, we were carefully yet deliberately sidelined. Memory asked us to celebrate History, and the media to consume it. Events had no place for us but that of spectator: we were erased.[3] It was far too much to ask in return for a life of peace and quiet. We wanted to dance, to get into the film before it was too late. Curiosity, in short, wasn't enough. A restless and impatient public refused to settle for existence as nothing more than an abstracted gaze. Anyway, why should we be excluded? We needed our share of pseudo-events: we got it by identifying with the famous insurgents parading across the screen, or those that collective memory produced.

Not yet fully at home with the image, we rejected the strictly contemplative posture the media had designated as ours. Embarrassed consumers of pleasure, we lived an obviously comfortable life as if it were some sort of persecution or pain. We looked at current events the way Emma Bovary read popular fiction: enraptured by escapism. We were shopgirls, longing for political romance. Like Emma, we carried on as if obstinate dreamers, shunning the morning light. We imitated images, not content to lose ourselves in them, gave our entire being over to them in complete surrender, satisfying an equivocal desire for escape (because we felt ourselves going stale from inaction) and expiation (because there was something obscene in casting a serene gaze on horrid events). Was this the easy way out? It remains the case that in order to gain access to reality or what went by reality's name, we were unable to find any other solution than to live in the imaginary.

Still, there were several false notes in this *symphonie fantastique*. Nothing really serious: two or three jokers who carped while we, swaggering princes at play, did our Don Quixote routine. Knock off the act, they said. "Cut the trickery: Quit trying to use theater to fill the gap between your inglorious, dull lives and the episodes that obsess you." Yet the din we raised was so great that such objections could scarcely be heard. Here and there, of course, diehards tried to dislodge us from the fiction that housed our revolutionary quarters, determined to drag us from plush environs our militancy was loath to leave. Were they more realistic than we? Far from it; they proved to be more deluded, more fanciful yet. Like us, they dreamed of History, or more precisely of Resistance and Revolution, everything else was worthless, dismissed as a sleepy waste of time. Hyperpolitical in appearance, they disdained "politics as usual" in the same terms as the average protester: in detesting the banality, delays and calculation of political compromise, they shared our nostalgia for the dark intensity of events that preceded our births. But our willingness to restage rather than actually relive such scenes was out of the question. The hard-liners hated posturing and prayed for an actual return of the past. We mouthed the standard stories as a token gesture, while their integrity demanded they be literally reproduced. Too cautious, perhaps, too inclined to satisfy ourselves with striking the right pose, we shared the same creed but flunked the test of intransigence. They failed us on the basis of our own principles. Confronting our longing for History, we had settled for a simulacrum. Worse than sacrilege, it was our crime, the unpardonable crime of refusing to shed blood. What did these apostles of apocalyptic struggle really want? Nothing less than exemplary loyalty to the mythology we espoused. Rather than hallucinate the antifascist struggle and revolution, we were to bend reality to our dream: only then, with History no longer unfurling in effigy, would we be cleansed of the sin of imposture. According to them, our hesitation made us clowns, charlatans – they reviled our prattle.

Take another look at *Dim Memories of a Polish Jew Born in France,* a book that exemplifies this "virile" disgust for frivolous agitation in the most gripping way. Is it because the author's expatriate father was both a Communist militant and a member of the Resistance? Pierre Goldman couldn't escape the hold of these memories from beyond the grave. With remorseless discredit, they struck a blow against every revisionist attempt.

> In Poland I was seized with a taste for action, overcome by the dream of, the desire for, history, and I wanted it to be a history of violence, in which I could free myself from the pain of being a Jew. I think I was also trying to recapture the time of my father, the time of my mother.[4]

Goldman, a loner and man out of season, is no child of his generation. Unlike his contemporaries, he couldn't be fooled. The times he struggled with all his might to revive belonged, as he himself put it, to his father and mother, an era that was at once familial and historical. This was an epic, spoken of daily in his surroundings, for which he felt a nostalgia touched with horror. Others, leftists, could go halfway, for they possessed only a bookish, approximate knowledge of these events. Not Goldman: his intimacy with the past ruled out mere simulation. The violence of the Holocaust enveloped him like a shroud, leaving him out of tune with the sixties, definitively estranged from their spirit of joyful play. The May uprising not only failed to end this rift, but made it still worse. No, Goldman was no child of '68 gone bad, as newspapers described him at the time, no student and participant in events at the Odéon who then took up a gun. The easy cliché-image of the leftist gone astray fails to define him for the good reason that Goldman hated the Left and never forgave the protesters their buffoonery and refusal to take up arms. Maladjusted, Goldman? True enough, but first and foremost a person who never fit in with the generation the press, for obvious reasons, wished him to symbolize. You never would have seen him at the front of a demonstration, chanting the childish slogan "CRS:SS."[5] With the Resistance as his sacred standard, Goldman was, in a manner of speaking, too pious to be satisfied with words. His turn to crime makes sense as an act of suicidal protest, leveled against the month of May and the verbal fairyland it became.

We all knew timid Jews, who would do anything to erase the slightest hint of their background. Goldman is also a Jew ashamed, but not of his Jewishness: he was afraid instead of failing to resemble the heroes of the concentration camps who haunted his memory. To superficial public opinion, those who cried in chorus "We are all German Jews" were his brethren. But while protesters slipped into an identity belonging to others, Goldman turned to crime in order to escape his own. In the History Store, the front window kept all victims of injustice on display. The protesters coveted the Jewish outfit, while Pierre Goldman, committing irreparable acts, sought to shed its garments once and for all. He passed from politics to armed assault because he never felt worthy of his heritage. As a mild-mannered, fortunate Polish Jew, he hoped to resolve this contradiction by committing violent acts. With this illusion shattered, he sought to chastise the traitor within, as if Judaism imposed an obligation to revolt that he had not known how to fulfill. Holdups were failed absolution, sanctions imposed for a kind of original sin: the crime of belatedness. Goldman punished himself for not living in Warsaw during the war, for knowing its brutalization only through stories or films. He consumed the Holocaust from his armchair, yet instead of experiencing a sense of relief – which would have been simply sensible – Goldman found himself guilty: delinquency was a self-inflicted penalty for living a deserter's life.

> A tribunal sat inside me, governed by a pitiless law, and before that tribunal I stood condemned only when confronted by my dreams, my ideals. Justice could not punish me, because, in my crimes, I had *already* punished myself. These crimes were not the offense of having stolen money by armed robbery. Rather, they were acts by which I had punished myself for not having been my father, a partisan, for not having been Marcel Rayman, for not having fought beside Che, beside Marighella, for not having tracked down Borman in order to kill him.[6]

Name is destiny: we know what befell the young Genet. One day while innocently committing a petty theft, a voice publicly informed him: "You're a thief." The name stuck forever, pinned him like a captured butterfly to his eternal truth. Nothing remained for him, only the task of carrying the adventure signified in his name to its logical end.[7] Goldman is Genet's opposite in this regard: his youth must have been passed waiting for a sentence that was never pronounced. In adolescence, he knew the strange frustration of never being labeled. The Other remained inscrutable; goys, rather than heckle him, obstinately kept quiet. For a time, the majority were actually silent and opaque. Goldman counted on ostracism. All he ever encountered was indifference. A would-be outsider, he was ready to assume his Jewish identity. What a waste of time! In his comfortable world, no hostile voice determined his fate. Goldman was equipped to counter prejudice, not to consent to silence. Others could be expected to do anything, anything but remain inert. And it was these unutilized Jewish faculties within that turned him to crime.

Since society had not disgorged him as a kike, he was forced – mysterious and ineluctable imperative – to exclude himself from Judaism. Turning himself into a criminal, Goldman took the position most diametrically opposed to the Jewish tradition. A bandit out of excess honesty? Whatever else may be the case, Goldman turned to crime simply because he couldn't stand being a *moocher* of the Jewish condition. A sedentary trespasser in the realm of sorrow and wandering, in a way he gave himself up, demanding the extradition due any clandestine traveler.

The judicial system, however, had a considerable surprise in store for him. In addition to his armed assaults, Goldman was accused of a double murder he didn't commit. He protested his innocence, all the while feeling a profound fascination for this crime that was not his own. Condemned to life imprisonment in 1975, he was in a way fond of this judicial error: paradoxically, the sentence acquitted him in his internal trial.[8] Goldman, who expiated his sense of insufficiency with aggression, and punished himself for being neither truly Jewish nor an actual combatant, acceded to Jewish dignity by taking on the combined forces of well-meaning types and "goyische justice" itself. The trial, which made him an authentic victim, joined the era he was forced to live in and the epoch of his obsession into one. The silent majority had been provoked into overreaction, giving him a renewed relation with "a specifically Jewish form of sorrow." In his calvary Goldman recovered the right to bear his name.

Did this strange act of consecration reconcile Goldman with himself? It was only after his sentencing, in any case, that he wrote his *Dim Memories*. The uproar produced by the work was important in bringing about his appeal. Tried a second time, Goldman was acquitted of the murder of the two pharmacists of the Boulevard Richard-Lenoir, and released several months later. He had spent more than six years in prison.

In writing about Goldman in this fashion, I had but one certainty: the case I was discussing was closed. This explains my eagerness, sometimes maladroit, to combine exposition with analysis, and while interpreting the whole to recount the major events of a story more than half-erased from memory and already out of date. After these lines were written, three killers plucked Goldman from obscurity, murdering him with nine bullets from a revolver, as if it were a parade. The stirring, mysterious life story of the Lost-Soldier-of-the-Revolution-become-a-gangster-who-redeemed-himself-later-by-becoming-a-great-author is once again a tale everyone knows. Was he good? Was he wicked? This serious question, resulting from the initial affair, had soon been displaced by another: French opinion was divided between those grieving for a writer and those for whom Goldman remained above all a thug. Devotees of his writing deplored the loss of a fine talent, for in France, since Villon, literature offers redemption for rogues, and a great work atones for every crime. The rest, closed to Goldman's prose, were surprised that so much clamor and uproar could be produced by what for them was only the logical conclusion to a sordid news item. Isn't violence the criminal's natural end?

On the Left, to be sure, we rebelled against the complementary clichés of criminal and artist. Barely dead, Goldman became a symbol for symptomatic social decay, a terrible presentiment of a future that was drawn in fascist hues. With every appearance of truth on its side, such discourse is powerful: a country where right-wing terrorism rages with complete impunity certainly does seem vulnerable to resurgent fascist groups. These fervent, self-assured Cassandras, however, were not quite believable, as they advanced their warnings from the wings: "This time *it's for real*! Fascism is here! We're in its midst, no deceiving ourselves now! . . . All the warning signs are there, all the indices say it's so. . . ." Far too eager and impatient, these prophets of doom remained unable to give their claims the force of truth. They salivated at the prospect of this blatant barbarity, greeted it with the violence of lovers too long deprived of the object of their desire, like actors burning to be back on stage after years of forced inactivity. Resuscitated and restored to a state of alert and of grace, they were bright-eyed and bushy-tailed, as in '68, happy to be able to play war and close ranks before a definable enemy once again. All the better that this fresh opportunity for confrontation had arrived, saving them from the stagnation of stale routine: melancholy without substance, implacable repetition, the absolute disarray of nothingness. When nothing is happening, we dream of catastrophe and think an increasingly fascist society preferable to no society at all. And in the night that obscures all targets, who doesn't feel nostalgic at times for a simpler world where, once and for all, absolute Evil could be torn limb from limb? Despite the fact that Goldman had made his life into a long, impossible battle against pretense, these flipped-out, thirty-something ex-lefties created a counterfeit fascism by shamelessly exploiting his death.

The import of the crime, of course, should not be minimized, or reduced, as so many well-intentioned people on both sides wished, to a mysterious case of settling old scores. Yet a society cannot be judged fascist on the basis of one act of terrorism. Nor is it justifiable to turn Goldman into the Cohn-Bendit case redux. We are not all Pierre Goldmans. This, by the way, no one dared mention, for as much as the crime might have troubled us, emotion rejected such pretentious words. A symbolic death? Assassination of a generation? No, Goldman died for none of us, stood in for none of us (that is, the "us" constituted by former protesters, the marginal, the Jews), but paid for his radical otherness. The killers liquidated all that was irreducible in him, everything beyond leftist agitation and classic militantism: the solitary vehemence that exposed this Jew by obsession, black by adoption and revolutionary to the vengeance of those for whom "France for the French" is at once a credo and worldview.

Goldman is no standard of failed protest: to the very moment of his death, he represented none but himself. As we went about our lives, Goldman devoted his to paying the infinite debt he owed the martyrs and survivors of the Holocaust, making his Jewishness powerfully concrete by living it as the obligation to challenge the world. This obsession isolated and distanced him from us, the children of '68, as we turned, in the guise of maturation, from imposture to compromise, from communitarian lyricism to blatantly individualistic pursuits. His murder moved us insofar as we were not its object, for it targeted Goldman's refusal to be satisfied with simulation and verbal insolence. Our reaction of muted rage could not be turned into positive political revolt. No slackness or passivity in this dejection, just a vague and irrational feeling of guilt, the sense that we had put as much effort into avoiding real danger as Goldman had expended in facing it, or more accurately, making it arise. Hence the deeper reason that his death galvanized so few of those it brought to suffer: no one had the heart to play cowboy *on that particular corpse*. To honor it required, before all else, this negative gesture: to not appropriate its difference.

It wasn't really our fault, of course, and uncomfortable feelings could easily have been rationalized away. To want one's life to measure up to the horror, no matter what the cost, why, you'd have to be crazy, that's for sure. For Goldman, a fortunate place in history was no consolation, he seemed to want an actual yellow star. As sensible types, we were protected from this morbid conflation of reality with fantasy, protected from any criminal temptation as well by an inaptitude for violence and the aversion it inspired. It never occurred to me, a Jew who experienced neither the persecution nor the war, to become a delinquent in order to atone for a comfortable life. But I've not always resisted the pleasurable temptation of claiming the victim's exemplary prestige as my own. Goldman has forever denied me this. His life was unique, beyond comparison, yet his refusal to act as if he were the heir to the sorrow, to live persecution at a comfortable remove, concerns all postwar Jews. I find in Goldman's story no capsule history of our generation, though here and there I'm called upon to do so – I see instead its disdain for bluster, and hear an amplified voice that whispers "Liar!" each time that, proclaiming my privilege, I make myself the spokesman of an accursed race.

Some on the Left thought they could speak for all the grand, oppressed subjects of the present and the past, and gave themselves license to impersonate them one by one. In following this pursuit, I thought I was living up to Israel's calling, and played the role of the Jew, the black, the colonized, the Indian, or the impoverished of the Third World. These were happy, boisterous years, when I stuck to my origins like glue. It doesn't work anymore; the drama's mainspring has unsprung. I'm an actor without parts, a laid-off tragedian. Even the affirmation "I am a Jew" quickly produces a painful sense that I'm *appropriating the Holocaust as my own,* draping myself with the torture that others underwent. Goldman helped me turn traitor and inform against myself. I have ceased making an innocent claim to the difference I possess.

There are those who, raised in religious orthodoxy, gradually begin to doubt and finally abandon the God of their fathers. I am an atheist of a different sort: having lived the cult of my Jewishness, I no longer believe in my own personal divinity. Not that I wish to renounce my origins, or even to mount an argument of my own for a policy of silence or assimilation. I am a Jew, its hold is inescapable: but no sooner have I written this than I sense a mistake, that an error in grammatical at-

32

tribution of person must have occurred. I am a Jew, yet the figure designated by this statement can be located nowhere – neither in the constants of my character nor in the biographical events of my life.

"The wandering Jew, that's me; the starving prisoner in striped pajamas, that's me; the little kid from Warsaw who faced the German machine guns, with a face of unbelievable seriousness and dignity, that's me once more; me, tortured by the Inquisition; me, the bloodied rabbi after a pogrom; me, Dreyfus on Devil's Island . . ." For the longest time, this is what Jewish identity meant in my eyes, and this, after years of bluster, is the meaning it has lost. A fundamental chasm exists between me and the history of my people, one I no longer seek to bridge. Having made so much of being a Jew, taken so much pleasure in using my ethnicity, uncovering, broadcasting and having it admired, the exhibition itself has become suspicious: I no longer believe that wishing upon a star makes dreams come true, or that self-puffery makes me an intrepid stoic at heart. The gullible days of my double life – when I could live the life of an average adolescent, and appear like a pariah or victim of oppression to boot – have finally passed. Their end has been a long time coming, yet it became absolutely necessary to bid farewell to the figure with whom I had confused myself. I divorced my double not to escape Jewishness, but so that Jewish identity would not turn me into a seigneur of suffering, or the appointed trustee of absolute justice. Jew, to be sure, but an *indebted* Jew (because individually, I am less, always less than what the term evokes), a Jew wishing to shed the theatrical patrimony where my roots had been struck. In Judaism I want to read something beyond pathetic affirmation, whose ostentation finally comes to naught.

Recent history has made people, probably no better or worse than the rest, into representatives of the Just. Ever since, the word *Jew* has been unable to take its place in ordi-

33

nary language, whether neutral or profane. *Jew* is a holy term: holy as in transcendent, inaccessible, in a realm beyond our grasp. This unapproachable name resists representation, remains apart from those who give it weight. The Jew may be our civilization's Other, but it is an otherness none can possess. To put it still more bluntly: the Holocaust has no heirs. No one can cloak himself in such an experience, incommunicable, if not the survivors. Among the peoples that constitute our generation, it is given to no one to say: I am the child of Auschwitz.

As an imaginary Jew, I have long lived my faithfulness to my Jewish background in a kind of appropriation, an innocent, pleasant time when Jewish destiny was mine to enjoy, as if I were its essence distilled – its emanation, monopolizer and symbol all wrapped up in one. Now I know that I am not a Jew in the same way I am dark, curly-haired, worrisome or timid. I no longer sustain a possessive relationship to Judaism; its history is neither my truth nor estate. In the noun that nonetheless designates my identity, nothing defines or belongs to me. To the question "Who am I?" the answer "Jew" is never a pertinent response. The past, from which I refuse to avert my gaze, reflects more than an embellishment of my looks. For if Judaism in fact has a central injunction, it should be thought of not as a matter of identity, but of memory: not to mimic persecution nor make theater of the Holocaust, but to honor its victims. That injunction is simply to keep this moment in Jewish history – which in no way means excluding contemporary reality – from conforming, banalizing and domesticating itself in history books, so that it does not gradually disappear into oblivion.

3
From the Novelesque
to Memory

I must acquire everything, not just the present and the future, but also the past, that thing of which every man receives a share free of charge; I must acquire that too, and this perhaps my most difficult task; if the earth turns to the right – I don't know if it does – I must turn to the left to catch the past. – Franz Kafka

To claim as my own: for many long years, this was my unique and glorious mandate. I was never one of the feckless who took the easier path, chose a French-sounding name and fled the burden of identity in silence or apostasy. "So what are you?" I never would have exploited the confusion that reduced Judaism to a religious category by replying to this question with: "Me? I'm an atheist, I don't believe in God." For me, atheism was no hideout, no pretext for an irreligiosity that would allow me to abandon my people for the free-thinker's cozy and peaceful confines. I was a Jew without God, but a Jew before all else. No conduct seemed more odious or degrading to me than that of the *turncoat*. My own frankness was the very opposite of such cowardice. By reclaiming my tradition I could beat my eventual aggressor to the punch, assert I was a Jew before another's malice could label me such. I was thus proud of my origins, and my Jewishness had no content beyond this wariness and pride.

The Holocaust I never forgot. On the contrary, I couldn't stop thinking about it. Deep ignorance, curiously enough, went along with this obsession. Why did I need to know every detail of how the Holocaust took place? A few family stories, indelible images from *Nights and Fog,* a number repeated interminably – six million Jews exterminated during the last war – were enough for me. The rest mattered little. Leave scholarship to the experts, my instincts were proof enough. Jewishness coursed through my veins, was my inner truth, my flesh and blood. The culture of the ghettos and scars of deportation still dwelled in the depths of my soul. My character had been molded by twenty centuries of suffering: I was one of the earth's living repositories of the *Jewish spirit.* I never would have thought of using the much maligned term *race,* and yet, imbued with the sensibility of my people, an authentic part of a larger process, a link in an uninterrupted chain of being, I pledged implicit allegiance to the determinism of racialist thought. Unwittingly, I followed Barrès. I could therefore do without memory, for Jewishness thought and spoke through me.

What I didn't see then was that by appropriating the Holocaust as my own, I mystified and softened its horror. Five years had been enough to destroy an entire civilization. It had disappeared. And while it wasn't courage or vigilance that brought me to face that fact, I acted as if I were one of the victims. Eager to assume responsibility for Jewish destiny, and wishing to stand by my people, I forgot this: they no longer existed. A disaster without precedent cut me off from Jewish culture, and I, a simmering rebel, reforged an artificial and reassuring continuity between present and past. I filled in the gap that held me distant from generations gone before. Because I was Jewish, I felt I had been born to a tradition of exile, but the Holocaust had exiled me from the experience of Jewish collectivity itself. Experiencing the travails of my people in dream, I denied this rupture; orphaned from Judaism, I wrote myself back into its genealogy and the trick was done: I had domesticated Auschwitz, turned the massacre into a strictly numerical and therefore a reparable state of affairs. Only sufficient effort would be needed to move beyond it: with fecundity, and a little time . . . At heart, my piety evinced a casual attitude toward the disaster, as if it were merely a painful parentheses in a story which, for all that, hadn't lost its thread.

Today, I would no longer rely on my Jewish spontaneity. I am nothing instinctively, unable to claim any specific kind of cultural difference. My gestures, language, habits, appearance and way of life have been washed clean of every particularity. In public as in private, I am identical to non-Jews, an impeccable likeness. Nor has such typicality been mine to choose or reject. It is the result of neither a fading culture in decline, the homogenizing power of capitalism, nor of progress and its ineluctable course. Could the West, that vast, elusive entity signified with a capital letter, be behind this leveling effect? Will we once again condemn, in absentia, the society in which equivalence rules? No. Jewish life was suddenly reduced to folklore by a specific, singular, and quite recent event: the Holocaust. Hitler's achievement cannot be diminished on the grounds that his task remained unfinished, and that he lost the war. The success of the extermination is measurable not just by the number of dead, but also by the poverty of contemporary Judaism. Chaïm Kaplan erred on the side of optimism when he wrote in his account of the Warsaw Ghetto: "Our existence as a people will not be destroyed. Individuals will be destroyed but the Jewish community will live on."[1]

Certain communities, to be sure, remain practically intact, those whom the Nazis' lethal violence was unable to reach. The rest belie Kaplan's prediction, and show that the opposite has come to pass. Only in numbers did the Nazis fall short, despite their monstrous toll of victims. While defeat prevented them from completing the final solution, they achieved a qualitative success: Yiddishkeit was erased as one of the world's unique cultures. That's why I, an Ashkenazi, am a Jew without substance, a *Luftmensch,* but not a beggar or wanderer in the traditional sense. Today's *Luftmensch* is the Jew in a state of zero gravity, relieved of what could have been his symbolic universe, his personal place or at least of one of his homes. To console myself, I always rehash the same subject: my profundity. I avenge myself in psychological complexity for the diaphanous slice of Jewishness I actually possess. If I can't be a member of a living Jewish community, I can devote myself at a moment's notice to the pleasures of self-interrogation: he who is deprived of Jewish ethnicity finds in the Jewish question endless food for thought.

The force of things has made me an introspective Jew, leaving me but a single faculty for escaping the monotony of the inward gaze: memory. Willed, laborious, faulty, untiring memory, a far cry from two thousand years of History at the tip of my tongue. Jewishness doesn't come naturally: an uncrossable distance separates me from the Jewish past. With the Jewish community carried off in catastrophe, my homeland is gone. Memory's imperative springs from the painful awareness of this divide. Unquenchable nostalgia for the Jewish life of Central Europe is the entire legacy I have been left. Jewishness is what I miss, not what defines me, the base burning of an absence, not any triumphant, plentiful instinct. I call that part of myself Jewish that remains at odds with life in its time, and which cultivates the powerful supremacy of what *has been* over what is.

> It happens that peoples lose their connectedness: it's a great loss, of course, and consolation is hard to find; but here comes Doctor Soïfer with his own loss to bear. . . . For he is one of those who are in the process of losing their people. . . .

38

What? . . . What's that he's losing? . . . We've never heard
of such a loss![2]

A young bourgeois, spared by History, feels a growing fascination for the times in which his people lived. Must such curiosity be seen as a return to roots? The image is tempting but
inexact: it conjures up hordes of former progressives, now
scouring bygone eras, waiting for the past to divulge the foun-
dational truth of the self. If only tomorrow could be like yesterday – those were the days! Genealogies have become the
rage, as everyone looks for the meaning that contemporary
life so cruelly lacks. Deep disillusionment has seized old devotees of the meaning of History; today, relish for one's origins has replaced the taste for revolt. The sickness specific to
this last quarter-century is the need for roots. But how the
devil would I go about tracing my roots in Galicia or prewar
Warsaw, knowing only a few curses and terms of endearment,
and two or three Yiddish and Polish turns of phrase? This
murdered world moves me, haunts me, precisely because I am
completely excluded from it. Instead of examining the past for
images of myself, I search for what I am not, what it is now impossible for me to be. Far from ending my exile, memory
makes it deeper by making it more concretely felt. No feeling
of recognition ties me to Poland's lost Jewish community. To
know it, to visit it repeatedly through books (the only locales
where it still exists), is only to measure my own estrangement
from what has been lost. These prewar Polish Jews brought
back to life by certain scholarly and literary works, these are
my people. Yet to sound, search and excavate my inner depths
would be in vain, no trace of them remains, except perhaps my
taste for poppy seed bread, scorching hot tea, and the way I
hold sugar in my teeth rather than let it dissolve. Tenuous and
fragile roots, to be sure.

What I have here called memory is thus the useless passion
a vanished civilization stirs in me. Not just useless, you might

say, but morbid as well. What's dead is dead. Why spend time energetically sifting through the ashes, when the effort would be better spent fighting for Jewish renewal or social justice? If only for this reason – and I offer it here in the name of a Jewish way of life, surrounded by its absence: that today, everything conspires to make us believe that such a civilization never existed. Everything: the uncommitted and their indifference, the pressures and everyday worries of contemporary life, and even the way our era remembers the Holocaust, however reverential it might seem. We spare no expense and produce an irreproachable commentary on these occasions, superlative heaped on superlative, choked voices and torrential sobs abound. The process of erasing the history of these people, so recently robbed of life, is apparent in two recent tearjerkers: *Holocaust,* the TV series judged to be worthless, and *Guichets du Louvre,* a film praised for its lucid intelligence.

Only two types of European Jew existed at the war's start: white, Western, normal ones, with the average man's clean-shaven look – and Jews from the olden days, picturesque throwbacks and medieval remnants, recognizable by their black caftans and sidecurls. The former spoke the majority's language with exemplary correctness; the costumed silhouettes, on the other hand, expressed themselves in Yiddish, and found nothing better to do as their hour of doom approached than to don their ceremonial shawls and sway rhythmically in prayer. Television will tell children what a Jew used to be: a figure constantly swaying back and forth. The image, of course, is hardly malicious: our era drips with compassion for these rockers-in-prayer, with no words harsh enough for the barbarians who put them to death. In guilty pity and its zeal, we're almost moved to think the world inhabited by those pallid scholars of the synagogue was Eden. Their swaying in prayer, we imagine, was a spiritual ideal whose like will not be seen again. More than bewail these psalmists in beard, we're meant to envy the wisdom we have lost, to grant them our compassion as a kind of homage. What can be said after such an orgy of goodwill? Simply this: that the opposition on which it rests is false. Between the wars, the Jews of Europe were anything but a homogeneous community, and certainly not a community divided in two, split between a group of doctors-lawyers-bankers and those who wore traditional garb. Yiddish was no exotic dialect, spoken by a few fossil throwbacks as the world left them behind. Three million Jews lived in Poland; their culture was a varied space in which the observant and the secular, Zionists and Bundists, Orthodox and Reform Jews, cosmopolitan citizens and inhabitants of the shtetls rubbed shoulders and confronted one another. You could keep the sabbath without looking like a bearded prophet, enjoy the Yiddish theater as well as Bizet's *Carmen,* study the Torah and play Ping-Pong or volleyball, be fully Jewish and reject the Talmud's rules. Modernity and Judaism were not the two mutually exclusive options, one set against the other, that we have retrospectively made them to be.

Even in our beloved France, Eastern European immigrants were so visibly Jewish that their coreligionists became uneasy. Assimilated Jews for the most part rejected these aliens who "vulgarly" betrayed their origins, while the assimilated, by contrast, outdid themselves trying to make their own Jewishness disappear. Everything about the newcomers spoke against Israel: accents, gestures, physical appearance – everything except their religious ways. Local craftsmen from Belleville, La République and the Marais truly enlarged the scope of synagogue architecture: classifiable as neither assimilated nor traditional, they remain absent from our reconstructions of the past. In *Guichets du Louvre,* a film devoted to their portrayal, they appear dressed in Levite coats, which they in fact never wore; while waiting for the police to raid, they sway in prayer, the perfect image of the Jew. In our desire to see clearly, we no longer see at all. We commemorate, in amnesia, the destruction of a nation. And so the Jewish people have been made to suffer a double death: death by murder, and death by oblivion. Collective memory reserves space only for those who look like we do, or for museum artifacts or circus freaks.

They're even better than the Mona Lisa, these Jews from another age: in portraying the actions and gestures of the ancient Hassidim, pathos is de rigueur. It all seems inevitable. By reducing Jewish life to something archaic, the Holocaust is implicitly defined as a rapid historical advance. Haste may be cruel and inhuman, but weren't they victims – those anemic scholars who studied, interpreted and chanted nothing but the sacred word – of progress itself? A death by natural causes for Jewish culture would of course be preferable. Hitler disagreed. The elegiacally inclined can still visit Mea Shearim in Jerusalem, or certain neighborhoods in Brooklyn and Anvers. There they will see those freaks in flesh and blood: our era's last representatives of the Jewish civilization of Central Europe.

This is our official cult of the dead, a debasing distortion. With an outpouring of tears we're offered the image of a senile community being put to death, when it was a vibrant, multi-faceted and creative culture the Nazis killed. Blatant indifference would surely do less harm than commiseration of this sort. For when all is said and done, and the public mind has been presented with the image of these helpless dotards – swaying, wasted bodies bemoaning their worldly woes – what else is there to think? Only that they were led to the slaughter in resignation, like docile sheep, and that they met their destruction with the calm and absolute passivity of those who firmly believe the Messiah will come. Religious hope doesn't foster the military calling, and you can't forge a resistance from people who sway over the prayerbook from dawn to dusk. By now, of course, the Warsaw Ghetto uprising has at-

tained universal recognition and even receives fervent celebra-
tion, as if to better emphasize its exceptional status. Good
thing they were there, the rebel few, to salvage, in extremis,
the honor of an anesthetized people! Such unique prowess,
moreover, is imputed spontaneously to those least Hebraic of
Jews, the aberrants, those already-Israelis, our alter-egos,
counterparts and brethren, who possessed the anticipatory
courage to shed superstition and its ancestral yoke.

It's tenacious, this legend of Jewish passivity, a vile myth
worse than oblivion. Victims of the Holocaust are treated as if
they *collaborated* in their own destruction. The ss were filthy
murderers, of course, but it must be said, must it not, that the
Jews – bewildered, taciturn and afraid – did their part. A suicidal propensity? Masochism? Scapegoat complex from time
immemorial? Did they render themselves unto God in a kind
of mystical fervor? Was accepting their fate their way of obey-
ing God's command, or did they refuse to face it in outright
denial of reality? While religion and psychology endlessly dis-
pute the key to the riddle, Auschwitz is gradually transformed
into evidence of man's dizzying capacity for passivity. No
longer the mystery of Nazi horror that piques the popular
imagination, but the far more exciting mystery of Jews who
failed to act.

> There was no way to escape these kinds of stories. Why
> didn't the Jews revolt? Why didn't they fight? Why didn't
> they form an Underground? Why were the Germans able
> to say: *Die Juden sind die billingsten und willingsten Arbei-*
> *ter?* The type of question you are asked by those with hearts
> of stone and eyes of ice.[3]

It's unbearable, this arrogant summoning of ghetto
dwellers and camp prisoners to answer before an abstract tribunal, a scandal. Yet for all our disgust, the indictment still requires a response. Jews who forty years ago suffered through

Hitler now need lawyers for defense. Today and for the fore-seeable future, we are reduced to justifying the victims for a massacre carried out against them. The task of rehabilitation rests with us, there's no escape: for Jewish memory is nothing but an incessant struggle we must wage against majoritarian memory, to reclaim the Holocaust's dead from the creeping conformism disguising them for posterity as confused and consenting prisoners put to death.

Oh, if only the children of Israel could have assembled a gigantic secret army in the Diaspora, instead of letting themselves be broiled in crematoria or forced to dig their own graves! Oh, if only a few Jean Moulins could have roused those pale, pious, skullcapped intellectuals from their rabbinic sleep! Similar expressions of astonishment are given utterance at every retrospective. The reasoning is idiotic, but impeccable: as long as you're condemned, why not die bravely, with honor and if possible as a hero. When you've got nothing left to lose, and still wish to retain your manhood, you don't go without a fight, without making them pay a heavy price for taking you down. But did the Jews of occupied Europe even know they were destined for death? Were they gorged with information, like today's unseemly inquisitors who grant them a dishonorable discharge, unafraid to fault the victims for their inferior will to fight? Had they seen films on Auschwitz, complete with visit to the gas chambers, estimate of their capacity, and description of cyanide gas and its effects? The Nazi high command itself did not receive the order to implement the "final solution" until January 1942, at the famous Wannsee Conference; some of the most hardened officials in attendance were stupefied by the incomprehensible news. In *technical* terms alone, it was beyond the reach of your average bureaucracy to go out and annihilate eleven million people! Machine guns were inadequate, nerve gas wasn't up to the task, carbon monoxide required a complicated system, and the furious

44

anti-Semitic propaganda of Hitler's early years had to be toned down. The artisans of execution would not meet the industrial challenge with more gun cartridges or inflammatory rhetoric. A qualitative break was required: mass murder demanded the gas Ziklon B and the mystification of its victims as well. In the gradual transformation of Polish concentration camps into extermination camps, bombast gave way to euphemism, and suave persuasion took the place that spiteful eloquence had held. Such rhetoric certainly remained a credible threat: the Germans hadn't promised the Riviera to the deportees, only assured them of "resettlement," or transfer to the East. A carefully monitored use of terms banished death from the Nazi vocabulary. Are the Jews guilty for letting themselves be fooled by this sanitized lexicon? Stepping outside our eminent position as judge for the moment, let's imagine the situation faced by internees from Pithiviers or Beaune La Rolande in May 1942, forced to leave their camp for an unknown destination in Eastern Europe. The prospect of slave labor stands before them. Isn't that terrifying enough? What else can the Germans do to them? "[Give them] another hole in the ass?"[4]

The attitude of those who believed they were being resettled in the East, when they were in fact being shipped to Auschwitz, need not be seen as naive, or blindly self-assured. From the onset of hostilities, Jews expected the worst from Hitler. The worst might be forced labor, maybe even slavery, the rounding-up of a nation to create a free, instantly disposable group of hands. But Hitler exceeded all expectations: he gave them *worse than the worst*. Jewish historical memory actively opposed the possibility that such systematic annihilation might be foreseen. The Jews were fooled, to be sure, but by their own pessimism more than anything else. Believing themselves experts in matters of persecution, the Jews had been lulled into a false sense of security by so much experi-

45

ence, all the more unprepared because they were so certain they'd seen it all. For two thousand years they'd done the grand tour of sorrow, become ultracompetent. The Nuremburg Laws? An attempt to reverse Jewish Emancipation and restore the Old Regime. The creation of the ghettos and the enforced wearing of the yellow star? Clearly a return to the Dark Ages. Every measure had its resonance; these experts in tragedy, it seemed, could never be caught unawares. In a history full of misery, having a name for everything bolstered Jewish confidence. They had no name for the Third Reich's policy: in Jewish culture, the Holocaust was an unprecedented event.

As powerless outsiders, Jews were used to outbreaks of hatred from the indigenous population, even bloody ones. They had served as decoys, safety valves for social unrest. Their presence soothed social frustration without, as it were, endangering order. As fodder thrown to the discontented, they were salvation for the State: the world needs its expiatory victims. Some communities, resigned to this sacrificial role, followed a strategy of keeping quiet and letting the storm blow over. For example, look at French Jewry during the Dreyfus affair. Steeped in centuries of persecution until it became imperceptible, Jews thought Hitler would follow the usual policy of victimization, when in fact he was about to invent another: extermination. *Scapegoats* from time immemorial were rudely cast into an unrecognizable world, subjected to total war and treated as the *absolute enemy*. How many Jews, confounded by their own clairvoyance, sought to deny the slaughter by thinking the Germans were just run of the mill anti-Semites, albeit of the most frightening kind! Ingenuity, they thought, would be enough to dissuade their executioners. Two millennia had been time enough to perfect techniques for getting by: bribing the authorities, becoming indispensable. But in wartime, such ingenuity served only to *normalize* their interlocutor, by crediting him with a language he didn't speak: the language of utility. Yes, today we know that the Germans acted against their own interests by eradicating an often irreplaceable labor force crucial to their war effort. If at first they liquidated the starving and useless, it was not – as they let it be hoped – to spare productive workers, but rather to avoid a glut in the system: they couldn't kill everyone at once; the slaughter had to proceed according to pace, be carried out in an orderly fashion. Countless "biological enemies" of the Reich failed in their first attempts to grasp the final solution's politics, for they deciphered its coded text with a key meant for other messages. Exhausted by the persecution and economic violence they'd managed to endure, they were hardly in a position to anticipate the gratuitous violence about to rain down on their heads.

It's about time we understood their *stupefaction* – Monday-morning warriors that we are – and quit reducing it to passivity! For those privileged to be victims of the Nazis, any clear view of their persecutors was obstructed by a historical barrier comprised of the hatred, verbal taunts and various kinds of lynching and enslavement they'd already endured. Jews had known duress for so long that Hitler's menace could only evoke a sense of déjà vu. Historical experience was deceptive, leading Jews to believe that they were on familiar terms with the unthinkable. Having passed through so many travails, Jews thought Nazism could be handled, and that it could be explained by one of the categories which cultural memory already possessed. In a kind of tragic quid pro quo, the condemned often confronted extermination with the useless responses that earlier persecution had taught.

But the methodical finality of Nazi violence had no precedent. Hitler was no frenzied mob leader and the ss, in their beautifully tailored uniforms, had nothing in common with the instigators of the pogroms. Too neat, too meticulous, too

47

well-trained, they were nothing like the Ukrainian or Polish looters the Jews were accustomed to seeing. There was doubt-less no shortage of German troops who were sadists, now able to unleash their blood-lust as never before. But the true execu-tors of the Holocaust, making it possible despite its enormity, were the farthest thing from perverts: they were model func-tionaries. Think of Eichmann or Rudolph Hess, Comman-dant of Auschwitz: while Jews knew barbarism only by its beastly face, and still expected violent rage, these bureaucrats dispatched their victims with a ferocity that was neutral, ad-ministrative, dispassionate and routine. Evil, they knew from still recent experience, was a spectacular and sporadic kind of disorder. It was the banalization of the crime that was incon-ceivable: the dull, methodical and continuous terror that the Nazis were about to make them endure.

The final solution effectively broke with anti-Semitic tradi-tion, replacing the savagery of the ancient saturnalia with dis-cipline and efficiency, those distinctive virtues of work. And we think the Jews should have known this, and mounted an effective resistance! We'll show them how it's done! We criti-cize them gently, but with a hint of irritation: "You must have been sleeping! Couldn't you have fought back against those disgusting animals, even a bit?" And here is the most amazing thing of all: the same people who indict the alleged passivity of the victims repeat their disbelief from a distance of thirty-five years and in spite of the accumulated information we pos-sess. Such prosecutors have learned nothing of the Holocaust. Like blind men, they castigate the Jews for being blind. Today we still refuse to grasp what we blame the prey for not being able to see: the mediocrity of the hunters, their dull and me-chanical impassivity. The "indefatigable little workers" (Musil) of extermination are depicted as if larger than life. We eroticize and bestialize their conduct, adorning it with the purple hues of decadence, or primitivism and its brilliant tints.

48

No longer technicians, they're monsters, Sadian heroes let loose in nature, Teutonic ogres wreaking their horrors while the music of Richard Wagner plays. Originary violence or the twilight of Evil: our era clings obstinately to imagery that the Nazis rendered completely obsolete.

Romantic or perverted executioners would have been incapable of carrying out genocide. A task of this magnitude called for qualities lacking any such notoriety: National Socialism brought rationality to the field of crime that was previously reserved to the industrial sphere. Its "managers" cannot be accorded any such complexity, whether it be sexual, unconscious or animal. These were heroes of maximum efficiency and absolute indifference, assiduous administrators whose only values were productivity and obedience. Barbarians, to be sure, but only in their excessive normality: they produced Jewish death with diligence and know-how, just as their contemporaries were experts at manufacturing medicine or automobiles. It would certainly have been comforting to attribute their unprecedented crime to human beasts, dangerous lunatics or visionaries. In fact, the most pitiless acts of inhumanity were committed by the most utterly ordinary men. The *disturbing familiarity* of the Holocaust lay in the fact that it was tailor-made for modern man, too civilized to participate in a *ratonnade,* a game for fools.[5] The sight of blood revolts him, and cruelty sickens him as soon as he sees it in the flesh. His delicacy is far better suited to the inherent abstraction of bureaucratic violence than to rage or to violent outbreaks suddenly unleashed.

With Hitler, to be sure, the Evil inflicted on the Jews reached a new level: more importantly, that evil was completely new in kind. The world's most powerful state plotted the disappearance of a people deprived of an army, land and allies. No one had ever waged such an unequal, total war, pitting a defenseless nation against another armed to the teeth.

Yet in spite of their amazement, and in spite of their impotence, Jewish partisans fought in every occupied country. There was the Warsaw Ghetto uprising, the thousands of Jews of Lublin, Lódz or Bialystok killed on the spot for refusing to obey an order, for insulting an SS officer, or striking him or spitting in his face. There were, of course, Jewish officials who thought they were saving themselves and their families by delivering a daily deportation quota to the occupation's authorities. In the ghetto's ashes, you even saw informers who led German soldiers to the bunkers the last survivors had dug. Yet at a time when all Europe lay prostrate under Hitler's domination, the mystery to be explained is not the resignation of the Jewish majority, but the fact that some chose to revolt. In the controlled climate of today's Europe, where no gesture has a price, we are all too eager to treat this rarity – the man who says no, and breaks with slavery – as if it were the norm.

But resistance and resignation are crude approximations, a rigid, Manichaean opposition that forces reality into distorting and dehumanizing terms. The masses who did not take up arms are not guilty of indolence or inertia. The Germans wanted the Jews dead; to stay alive, Jews had to demonstrate ceaseless and feverish *activity*. Rather than rise in suicidal revolt, they opposed their killers through ruse. Not by giving in, but by an infinite dexterity in all the shady dealings that governed ghetto life: countless forays to the Aryan side (where a swarm of Poles, much more than the SS, were virtuosos at fingering a Jewish face in the crowd); contraband to feed the people even while the Nazis sought to starve them to death; a tight network of clandestine institutions to sustain, whatever the cost, the community's sense of solidarity; flour mills for bread in hidden cellars and attics; tiny orchards on roofs or balconies; a low rate of suicide, proof, at the very heart of hell, of an unbelievable will to live. Such efforts and minor stratagems for survival are nothing very spectacular in themselves, far from the heroic scenes of a war epic. In the face of the German steamroller, they were often without effect. But only ignorance born of comfort and virile fanaticism bring our time to scorn such acts, and read them as variants of a uniform and degrading passivity.[6]

Those who chose the path of rebellion, moreover, were not members of the Resistance in the classic sense. They didn't wage war, like partisans whose sabotage, espionage and guerrilla raids weakened the occupier and helped the Allies in their task. Unlike the maquisards, they didn't supplement conventional forces engaged on the battlefield. The Jewish resistance fought a lonely and useless fight. The ghettos and camps are the only places where resistance and the hope of survival were pitted *against* one another in such a tragic way. For the insurgents, victory was like the promised land, and rebellion made it virtually certain they would never reach its bounds. To revolt was to prefer certain death to the chance, itself minute, that you might hold out until Hitler's defeat. For this to be possible, a person's will to escape or to triumph had to be weaker than the wish to bear witness, and thus shame the world for its *apathy* in the face of disaster.

Where then did the true scandal, true passivity reside? In the procession of the deportees who accepted an atrocious death without striking a blow? In the supernatural calm of the sons of Abraham? Or rather in the indifference that the overwhelming majority of their contemporaries displayed before the machinery of annihilation? Wondering how the Jews could allow themselves to be abused raises the fundamental question: how was the rest of the world able to allow the abuse? Passionate questioning of the condemned and their silence points to the *other silence*: the silence of peoples who witnessed the Holocaust, of the Church, of Allied governments, of the media and of the Resistance, hardly in a hurry to come to the aid of people who could be of absolutely no use. Is it widely known, for example, that the main topic of public discussion in Poland just before the war was the emigration of the Jews? A question of central importance, more important than the German menace in the eyes of a majority of Poles. This wish for a homogeneous society, given explicit formulation throughout the 1930s, was fulfilled by Hitler's brutal style and the organizational genius of his administration: Make them leave! Make them disappear! Or is it widely known that immediately after the war, when barely fifty thousand of Poland's three million Jews had survived, pogroms broke out in Kraków, Kielce, Chełmno and other cities? Is it widely known that the Jews of the ghettos had the greatest difficulty obtaining arms, because they had no government in exile to represent them, and because their strategic worth was nil?[7]

The world has seen other genocides since the war. Only vanity would claim moral privilege or a monopoly on extermination for the Jews, for in this domain the Nazis were precursors rather than exceptions to the rule. Something unique, nonetheless, remains specific to these four years of dereliction, and it is not, as the familiar cliché would have it, the victims' resignation. "Unique in 1940–1945 was the abandonment," as Emmanuel Levinas writes. No petitions then, no press campaigns; no media to "cover" the Holocaust, no march, no swaying of public opinion. Not a sign from the world outside. An impenetrable wall, made of hostility, detachment, skepticism or ignorance stood between the suffering and those beyond. It is useless to cover up this silence with impenitent blather about Jewish passivity: it remains as dizzying, as incomprehensible today as it was forty years ago.

✧

It's natural these days to look ahead. "Onward" is the word on practically everyone's lips. Eccentrics who look back must explain themselves. Nostalgia must give meaning to contemporary life, must be of use here and now; preoccupation with the past must be part of a triumphant vision of the time in which each of us pays homage to a future that rules supreme. Consider the arguments that those who refuse to forget the Holocaust, wanting to retain a link with their vanished culture, are compelled to use. Memory, they claim, is nothing but a form of vigilance: "Of course we return to the past, good people, it's this very obsession that keeps us modern: it's our way of assuring that such a past will never return." Some zealots of modernity reject the excuse; the Jews, they say, open old wounds out of complacency, create a distraction. They say: Jews who harp on the Holocaust by continually bringing it up draw our attention away from crying injustice and more pressing instances of genocide. Such modernists blithely compare Jews of today with yesterday's anti-Semites: the former are said to dwell on yesterday's disaster when their efforts would be better spent facing up to contemporary history, just as the latter used racial hatred to divert social unrest that might have shaken the very foundations of capitalism itself. If one were to believe these censors of memory, today's honoring of Auschwitz is carried out for the same reason that hooked-nose parasites were hated before: to exorcize collective violence, using fictional unanimity directed against a helpless enemy to mask real social conflicts beneath. The Elders of Zion gave shelter to those responsible for human misery: of course, every memorial of the Holocaust serves to mask the torture chambers of Uruguay, Chile, or Argentina, if not refugees from Indochina, the Soviet gulags or unemployment in France. Thus, during the broadcast of *Holocaust,* few were the critics who brought out the film's deficiencies (and notably the total absence of Jewish life): innumerable, on the contrary, were the editorials that denounced it as a dangerous distraction. The time is past, they cried, to bewail the plight of the Jews. Make way for the Young! Make way for a new class of the damned!

The partisans of Jewish memory declare: The dead teach the living, warn them and open their eyes. The enemies of Jewish memory declare: These dead serve no purpose, weigh us down, enfeeble our vision, mystify what's at stake today. Both sides can conceive of the dead only in terms of their *usefulness*.

As for myself, I too spent all of my long adolescence making use of the dead. Shamelessly annexing them to myself. Voraciously appropriating their destiny as my own. Gorging myself on their agony. Now I know that memory does not consist in subordinating the past to the needs of the present, nor in painting modernity in dramatic hues. If the future is for all things the measure of value, memory has no ground: for he who looks to gather the materials of memory places himself at the service of the dead, and not the other way around. He knows that they have only him in the world, and that if he turns his back to the manner in which they lived and died, then these dead Jews who were at his mercy will truly perish, and modernity, in love with itself, absorbed by daily intrigues, will not even notice they have disappeared.

PART TWO

The Visible and the Invisible

4
The Jew and the Israelite: Chronicle of a Split

And when the father discovered in his child one of those words, one of those gestures that he knew well because they belonged to his grand-fathers, he told him: "Don't do that, it's Jewish." – André Spire

They exaggerate. They blow the whole thing out of propor-tion. Boisterous, utopian, boasting about Einstein, the Israeli Defense Force and the kibbutzim, they no longer know how to blend in. Their passionate attachment to Israel and insis-tence on being different makes them neglect their native coun-try: they *snub* France. Militant Zionism and their constant proselytizing of Israeli culture makes them act as if they were internal aliens. Is it because History has made them untouch-able? Whatever the reason, they're arrogant and gradually be-coming susceptible to sectarian lures: with God or without, the idea of being a chosen people once again casts its noxious spell. Look at them: drunk with a feeling of uniqueness. They are seriously lacking in the necessary reserve; the dangers such excesses pose to national unity and their own security have yet to cross their minds. These people who envisage paying taxes to a foreign power while flaunting their excessive feeling of community – are they truly citizens of France? Pride of caste and dual allegiance make them a nation within a nation, and such separatism is doubly unhealthy, for it weakens the state

57

and disturbs society as a whole. If this trend continues, the limits of tolerance will soon be reached: the Jewish question, papered over until recently by images of the concentration camps, will become explosive once again.

You'll already have recognized the outlines of the well-known argument recently developed by Alfred Fabre-Luce, in his pamphlet with that disarming title: *Ending Anti-Semitism*. Sensing that Jews as well as France faced trouble on the horizon, the celebrated historian knew the time had come to cry "Danger!" His book is a text written out of love and compassion, a wake-up call directed by a concerned humanist to a minority group he admires, but whose members are touchy, chauvinistic and heedless of the danger they court. With the intrepid pride of an iconoclast, a taboo-smasher, Fabre-Luce makes the daring claim that Jews are partly responsible for the hostility they provoke. Like a friend offering advice, he asks Jews to heal themselves of separatism as quickly as possible, before it's too late – before a new wave of hatred once again overwhelms our beloved land. In return for this display of good citizenship, the responsible majority of non-Jewish French would protect their Jewish fellow citizens against secular threats and would fight with every last ounce of strength any oblique or open move to make the people of Abraham scapegoats for social unrest once again. For anti-Semitism is just like marital strife: to get along, both parties have to meet half way. You must practice give-and-take. If not, cease-fires are a possibility, but any true and lasting reconciliation is out of the question. If the Jews would only know their place, get their arrogant, loudmouth leaders to pipe down, the rest of the citizenry would be reassured by such proof of national discipline and would quit believing in anti-Semitic rumors or ideas.

This minor guide to good conduct raised an almost universal hue and cry in the press, an amazing scandal if we are will-

ing to consider it in historical terms. For Fabre-Luce is no
Barrès, no Céline, no Maurras, and despite what might have
been said, his book claims no place in the tradition of French
anti-Semitism. There's no talk of Christ-killers; racist motifs
and the notion that capitalism is Jewish are foreign to his
thought. The absence of these three condemnations (biological, political and religious), moreover, is hardly a result of
careful word choice: good Jacobin that he is, Fabre-Luce is no
hate-monger but *an advocate of assimilation*. He calls upon
French Jews to embody those virtues they've imposed on
themselves for a century and a half: order, loyalty, discretion.
"Be a Jew on the inside and a man on the outside." Until quite
recently, this maxim attributed to Moses Mendelsohn was the
credo of every Jewish community in liberal Europe, the watch-
word of their lives. Your God is your business, a private affair,
a family matter: pray as you like in private, wrap tefillin once
again, speak to the Eternal One in the Hebrew language. But
fit in with the crowd when in public: be French in France,
German in Germany, ready to defend your country against
any foe. Be happy to die on the front lines, dedicated to repub-
lican government under parliamentary democracy, or a faithful subject in monarchies.

Fabre-Luce, while concerned for the state, doesn't ask
nearly so much. His recommendations are far less severe than
the severity that Western European Jews, at least, have shown
toward their own culture. As exposé, his work certainly is no
revelation of deep-rooted, classic anti-Semitism, or even a
sign of Petain's eventual victory in a France decidedly partial
to the past. The book and its reception are testimony to a revolutionary cultural shift: anti-Semitic discourse and the discourse of assimilation are no longer opposed – their status for
more than two centuries – but have been merged into one. A
fundamental change has taken place, as the Jewish question is
being played out from a new deck of cards: just thirty years

ago, anti-Semites considered Jews to be a stateless people, no matter how hard they struggled to join the nation as a whole. Today, the demand that Jews give up their collective identity is itself considered anti-Semitic – an unfair price to pay for wanting to be French like everyone else, or to feel a sense of belonging, whether it is made arrogantly or couched in kinder terms. The venerable concept of assimilation, the official policy of the past, has finally become unacceptable.

The story sounds like a romance novel. The Jews fell in love with the land of the Rights of Man, and were married; the all-consuming passion soon made them despise everything unique about themselves. They left it all behind to gain their lover's esteem, but the highest hopes of fitting in ran afoul of reality. Confronted with hostility that never subsided and even increased in strength, enthusiasm waned: the magic was gone, replaced by politics. Idealism degraded itself to become pusillanimity or opportunism, and conformity came to be seen as a condition of social success – nothing less than that, but certainly nothing more. All that remained of the original passion was a marriage of convenience. Today we live out the final scenes of that grand and shattered idyll. In their maturity, Jews have abandoned the strategy of self-effacement, for it seems at once illusory and despicable. They condemn assimilation, their sainted patroness, having discovered, behind her supportive allures, the contemporary face of anti-Semitism itself.

> *Let the Jews find their Jerusalem in France!*
> – Napoleon

Those emissaries of justice who suggested the Jewish minority could use a bit more restraint – suggested for their own good, of course, and out of devotion and philanthropic motives – have lost all credibility. We've become so adept at spotting intimidation and coercion in their smarmy benevolence that it's no longer easy to see assimilation as the seductive adventure it once appeared. Yet it was such an adventure, and something more than that: a kind of religious passion. French Jewry believed in the emancipation that the Revolution, for all intents and purposes, had finally brought them, and in the moral superiority of the nation that opened its doors. They madly venerated the people who were delivering them from bondage: full acceptance by French society was an article of faith. France was their bride, and assimilation their dowry, placed on the table with the rest of their gifts. This transformation of the Jews, their normalization, cannot be explained as a result of force. For it was not external pressure that obliged them to loosen their hold on idiosyncratic and overly mystical rituals or cultural traditions. The first Jews out of the ghetto, to be sure, were seized with fright at the prospect of emancipation and rejected the new order of things, afraid of the unknown, particularly the public schools, the army, and having to confront the world of the gentiles directly, without relying on the rabbis as a mediating force.[1]

But one or two generations sufficed to sweep away such hesitation: fear was followed by fervor, diffidence by sameness. In less than a half-century the French Jews left Judaism utterly transformed: the life that had been a daily routine for two thousand years was now a subjective belief, a religious choice. Accepting the Enlightenment's mighty oppositions of public and private, church and state, this "peculiar nation with its idolatry of law" (Rousseau) attacked its peculiarities and reformed its rituals, customs and observances. Austere rules governing actions sacred and profane were effectively abandoned. Worship became the singular form of religious life. The style of worship, moreover, began to copy Catholic rites. Like the mother who fends off old age by acting like her daughter's child, imitating her look, wearing the same jeans and buying the same perfumes, the synagogue modernized itself by following the Christian lead. Hence the organ was introduced to services; the rabbis, true Jewish priests, acquired the habit of attending sick at their deathbed and wore a costume almost identical to a priest's; baptism became widespread; the bar mitzvah, a ceremony of religious initiation for thirteen-year-old boys, looked more and more like Catholic first communion; the Chief Rabbi of France even gave brief consideration to holding Sunday services, in order to cut into the number of Saturday absentees.[2]

We can smile at all these cosmetic repairs, and even find something servile about them. We would love for these Jews to have displayed the stubbornness and pride that's distinguished their history so many times before. Why did this stiff-necked people suddenly become so flexible? Why the rush to become Christian? What good does it do to remain a Jew if Judaism reduces itself to a spiritual shell, nothing but a feeble copy of the dominant religion?

Such bold and impressive contempt for compromise, however, ignores the underlying force behind assimilation: the Jews' headlong dive toward modernity was activated by the profound sense of *appreciation* they felt. The long and complex history of the Diaspora had certainly included its peaceful oases, prosperous enclaves, privileged locations where good relations with the native populace had been sustained, whole periods when welcoming states enabled the Jews to let down their guard. But 1789 was still a powerful first. Never before had a nation granted citizenship to the Jewish community as a whole. It was not calculation but gratitude that determined the behavior the descendants of Moses displayed in response. To blend in with the French people, everything in their law that might mark them as strangers to the human community was cast aside. Jewish national identity was quickly sacrificed. Judaism slipped quietly into the depths of private life. Guilty of conformity? Far from feeling at fault, Jews at the time experienced the pleasant self-certainty that goes along with acting justly and keeping faith with the most fundamental moral law: they acquitted their debt by dejewifying themselves; the law, *their* law demanded they become mimics, for the advent of emancipation had placed them in France's debt.

That's right, we said appreciation: for gratitude was supported and shaped by a feeling of identification. Not only did the people of the Book lack any sense of betraying their mission or its history; the Revolution had been prefigured by no less exemplary a precedent than the biblical tradition itself. "Here is our second law from Sinai," Isadore Cahen wrote at the time. Maurice Bloch would speak of a messianic epoch; and then there was Rabbi Kahn: "It's our Exodus from Egypt, our modern Passover." No alternative presented itself. There was no agonizing choice to make as the process of assimilation began. Nothing along the lines of: if becoming a deserter is what it takes to achieve equality, it's worth it. These newly minted citizens saw no need to renounce their heritage in order to become French. By holding fast to Jewish culture, they became patriots. For it was as heirs to the prophets of Israel that they embraced the Revolution's cause. Light of heart, with the joy of duty well done, they forged a new kind of man, *the Israelite*: reserved, distinguished, conscientious and smitten with love for France.

But what of the transgressors? The visible Jews, those who stood out? Who spoke French with a bad accent? Who were nostalgic for the ghetto and rejected integration? And the incorrigibles who persisted in acting as if a Jewish nation might still exist? Woe be unto these hardheads! Shame on their stubbornness! By unilaterally violating the rules of emancipation, they encouraged anti-Jewish sentiment and placed the safety of their coreligionists at risk: traitors twice over, they were inadequate as citizens of France and as Jews. For the Israelites, acting Jewish *in public* could only be seen as a kind of dangerous sabotage. Both morality and the more down-to-earth needs of security told the Israelites to remain aloof. To completely rid themselves of any distinguishing marks. To avoid those frequent confusions between upstairs and downstairs – between picture-perfect little Jewish citizens and inveterate pawnbrokers – by refusing any gesture of solidarity and becoming the most strident voice denouncing the unredeemable depravity of other Jews.[3]

For assimilation shared an implacable logic with the adventures of socialism to come: lofty idealism soon gave way to denouncing traitors to the cause. To have merely been an Israelite, happily staying out of the spotlight, to have remained a citizen beyond reproach with absolutely nothing bad to say about Jews who fit the images of popular stereotype – this would have left half the work of social integration undone. The caterpillar would have stayed shut in its cocoon; to become a butterfly, the legend of Jewish solidarity had to be given the lie. A shift from silence – a sign of toleration, or worse, complicity – to an accusatory stance had to be made. Whether it's communism or emancipation, new identities can be fashioned only by cutting all ties between the old man and the new. And since there are always holdouts who reject the movement, enthusiasm and personal sacrifice aren't enough: forms of policing are required, like informing, that indispensable aid to repression. The man of the past must be rooted out relentlessly: it's a question of life and death. The hunt demands a continual state of alert, for not to pursue him in others is an indirect admission that he still lives within ourselves. A revolutionary who defends the bourgeoisie, or tolerates its existence, is no indulgent revolutionary. This would be a contradiction in terms. He himself remains bourgeois. The same pattern holds for the Israelite: his regeneration and recovery cannot be regarded as finished until he devotes himself to an undying hatred of traditional Jews. Unless you join the battle against the lukewarm, timid and indifferent members of your race, you're hardly a patriot, and only a halfhearted citizen of France.

Angelic informers, idealistic police: such were the apostles of the Franco-Jewish betrothal. They were made for romance, not vile deeds. Their primary calling was poetry, not snitching on friends. Yet the fatal set of forces that made assimilation possible pushed them toward anti-Semitism as well. Wishing so desperately to become respectable citizens – after so many centuries of uncertainty and discrimination, a legitimate desire to be sure – and end prejudice once and for all, they became its practitioners. Was there any better way to disarm suspicion than to take it upon themselves to become the Jewish people's fiercest critics?

"You don't like the Jews? Neither do we! You think they're excessive in this, and deficient in that, too business-oriented to really be trusted; you think they're not refined enough for your taste? So do we! And while you're at it, please note that we take every possible opportunity to distinguish ourselves from their way of life. We may call ourselves Israelites, but we do it precisely to show how different we've become, and to erase, even in our language, whatever common bonds we still share. Please don't judge us too quickly – don't think of us as Jews, that stateless people in those bizarre costumes!"

Judeophobia among the assimilated was all the more passionate: their social status was at stake, living as they did under the constant threat of being identified as Jews. Impeccable behavior had been useless: society's hostility would never really disappear. Its paradoxical persistence was the fault of their burdensome coreligionists, those foreigners who refused to fit in. Innocent themselves, the assimilated were tired of paying the way for others. Feeling they had been done an injustice, they self-righteously sought redress. Hatred or disgust for Jewish difference became a natural part of being an Israelite.

Such difference, it must be understood, in Judaism extends well beyond the limited scope of the private sphere, and includes everything that meets the eye: gestures, sign language ("A Jew expresses himself as much with his fingers as with his tongue; single-handed, he would surely be half-dumb!"[4]), the shape of the face, dress, pronunciation, the religious injunctions one must follow each day . . . The only good Jew was an invisible Jew. The other, the visible Jew, was an obscene creature, indecent: morality as well as personal hygiene demanded that such an exhibitionist be shunned.

It all began around 1840 with a question of vocabulary. A few Israelite writers, exercised by what they believed to be a terminological confusion, asked that the adjective *Jewish* be stricken from the dictionary. Such a pernicious word had no right to live, for it evoked a dead reality, stood as a blemish, as their fellow French citizens saw it, on the Mosaic faith. The necessary and perhaps sufficient condition for ending anti-Jewish hostility was to make the word *Jew* – a distillation of venomous passion, a diatribe, a calumny – disappear. Israelites of that problem-free era were still preoccupied with escaping their past. There was no better target on which to vent their fears than those quaint phantoms and various types of the wandering Jew so popular in the literature of the day. Local color was the literary fashion: such folklore, and a far from conservative lexicon, provoked their rage. These were everyday people, not Shylocks or Wandering Jews concealing their evil deeds behind a bourgeois mask. And so the battle was limited to an abstract and conceptual plane: the new sons of France directed their anger at an adjective whose day was done.

Forty years later the word became flesh and the enemy was more than an image: the first Russian Jews to flee the pogroms began arriving in France. Real Jews had suddenly burst onto the scene, out and out Jews, blatantly Jewish, a sight that had become increasingly rare in Western Europe. The number of arrivals was small, it's true, but only a few Yiddish-speaking commoners were needed to bring panic to some and anxiety to the rest. For all the dignity of their starched collars, the Israelites were haunted by a single, horrifying thought: the immigrants' bad manners would be a disgrace. It was not just the fact that the presence of Ostjuden would disturb the non-Jewish populace; but they seemed intent on making coexistence impossible, with their strange dialect and the bizarre complexity of their culinary rites. On top of that, these mongrels had come at a bad time, however pitiful their plight may have been in those medieval lands they left behind; for France and Russia were in the process of forming a military alliance. By asking their coreligionists for hospitality or even help, the exiles threatened to ruin the social acceptance Jews had won at so great a cost. The Jewish community passed this patriotic test with flying colors: it gave hesitant welcome to a handful of refugees who claimed to be brethren, while four Parisian synagogues prayed for the health of Alexander III when he fell seriously ill in 1894. Alexander III – the bloodthirsty czar, a fanatic anti-Semite and distinguished technician of persecution, to whom we owe the appearance of the *pogromtchik,* this Jew-killing cop, orchestrator of the "spontaneous" uprising against the monopolists – this was the Alexander III whom official representatives of French Judaism honored in their own places of worship! It's a fact.[5]

After World War I, France rediscovered its lofty principles and tradition as a land of asylum. One reason was surely that the carnage had left the size of the French work force cruelly reduced. As a result, the severe labor shortage brought Jews from Hungary, Lithuania, Russia and Poland to Paris in droves. French Jews responded to this sudden influx of foreigners with an outcry of complaints and a gamut of grievances that is simply amazing. These untutored *Polaks* (as they were generally called) followed backward customs, were never on time, and of course their worst affront: in the land of wine, they drank tea! This outrageous insult was the straw that broke the camel's back. France had been hit where it hurts, in its gastronomic heart! Xenophobia, in a word, took precedence over solidarity for many Israelites, for they felt closer to their fellow citizens than to their fellow Jews. They were disturbed, even offended by these pockets of Yiddishkeit in the very midst of liberal civilization, erupting like boils on a delicate skin.[6]

And so the epic of assimilation took its course: not the progressive elimination of prejudice, but its extension, on the contrary, to the Jewish minority. Israelites had to be experts at imitating the Western model while simultaneously rejecting those of their kind who refused it, or those who simply lacked the means. Such a presence could only remind the Israelites of the fragile vanity of their own attempts. Sooner or later, the assimilated would have to pay for what these others had done and be mercilessly returned to the outsider status they were so proud to have left behind. There was only one way to counter the threat of this *judicial error*: to become judges themselves.

All for nothing – all the moral degradation and Jewish anti-Semitism for nothing: for the Holocaust. All the unpleasantness so willingly stomached, the nationalist promises, all the barriers erected between those foreigners and local Jews, the absolutely pathetic obsession with fulfilling their duty to France – all that, only to arrive at the tawdriness of the gas chambers. For the Nazi way of death, as we know, drew no distinctions between different kinds of Jews. Martyrdom unified a community sundered by 150 years of assimilation and its stress. Rich and poor, orthodox and atheists, the intractable as well as the conformists, the spineless and stiff-necked alike were snatched up pell-mell in its grasp. The catastrophe of conscience never saw the compensation of success: the Israelites never gained the material security they had sacrificed their integrity to achieve. The same people famed for their business acumen had struck a bad bargain with emancipation. The hour of their reckoning gives the predominant impression of being one horrible mess.

> *The smooth, dissolving hand of the hypocrite and the traitor.*
> – Drumont

Assimilation was more than just an ineffectual disgrace. Temptingly easy as it may be to stress its failure, to do so misses the truly *tragic* dimension of the assimilationist quest. We hear it all the time: what good was all their superpatriotism, their self-discipline, what did manners and polish do for them in the end? What good was studious application and frantic mimicry, since anti-Jewish feeling never subsided, and with Hitler even reached its peak? Jews say the same thing among themselves: "Let's quit being nice, acting like trained monkeys, like faithful dogs waiting for assimilation, the treat that never comes, the exam we always have to retake. Instead of cramming nonstop to pass, let's stop treating non-Jews as if they were Professors of the subject of France; the majority will always feel a certain and persistent mistrust and enmity with respect to our community. Anti-Semitism will never die." It seems the most lucid and thoroughly disillusioned position one could take.

But this journey to the bounds of bitterness still skirts the actual horror. Assimilation cannot be reduced to a *fiasco* pure and simple; it should perhaps be thought of as something more ironic, more diabolical yet: as a dreadful *misunderstanding*. Genocide was not imposed on the Jews *in spite of* their effort to assimilate, but *in response* to this very attempt. The more they hid their Jewishness, the more terrifying they became to others. As Jewish appearances gave less and less hint of ethnic background, the evils charged to Jews by anti-Semitic opinion grew worse and worse. Could these men of the Enlightenment ever have imagined that their increasing resemblance to the gentiles would arouse a hatred that ran so deep? They persuaded themselves it was their remaining Jewishness that their enemies attacked, when in fact it was their new stature that provoked rage and fear. The Israelites painstakingly cleansed themselves of every Hebraic trait; the reaction to this cultural stance reached a level of radical animosity far beyond the revulsion that inhabitants of the ghetto had come to expect.

For the myth of Jewish omnipotence to take hold, the people of Zion first had to pass unnoticed, merge with the general populace. It took a Jew without qualities to fit the part of spy or conspirator. Dreyfus, that patriot and devoted soldier, now he really looked like a traitor. Assimilation thus became a strange kind of trial in which the defendants completely misunderstood the indictment their judges had prepared. Assimilated Jews thought they were being charged with excessively Jewish behavior, when it was their will to integration that was really the crime: the wary would only weaken their case in the very way they secured their defense. A kind of relentless mechanism had been set in place, turning every protestation of innocence into yet more evidence of guilt.

Unwavering, the Israelites attributed their constant danger to those slovenly Jews, unwilling to assimilate, whose crassness and chauvinism reflected unjustly back on them. The reality was quite different: every time a poor, defenseless Jew was insulted, attacked or killed, it was always done to avenge those imaginary misdeeds, deviously committed in secret by the Israelites, the invisible people.[7]

The origins of this misunderstanding lay in the belief in *Progress*. Along with most of their contemporaries, newly emancipated Jews took it for granted that Reason worked itself out in history. Such teleological optimism reduced barbarity to an archaic remnant, and regarded Evil as a violent form of stupidity or error. Intolerance would wreak its depredations in vain: for these inheritors of the French Revolution, it was merely a symptom of the past. Everything would turn out just as it had in Mozart's *Magic Flute*: superstition and Enlightenment had fought their climactic battle, with anti-Semitism taking the side of obscurantism and outmoded beliefs. In any case, Jew-haters were mostly illiterate and gullible types brainwashed by the Church; increasing knowledge, the very movement of history since 1789, would sweep away their imbecilic clichés. Passé and out of touch, the wicked would have their hands full just holding on. Their days were numbered. Slowly, no doubt, but inexorably, rationality would lay fanaticism to rest. It was a matter of social maturity, no more and no less. So long as they steeled themselves with pedagogy and patience, the Israelites would pass the time well – justice and the future were on their side. Social acceptance was both right and inevitable (for the logic of Progress demanded it: the fortuitous fusion of the necessary and the good). In modernity's euphoric self-image, anti-Semitism was like the plague or a case of scabies, a disease medical advances would soon be able to cure.

Until Auschwitz and even beyond, Western Jews had placed their hopes in the progressive cause. New outbreaks of anti-Semitism were described as examples of backwardness or as lingering residues of the past. Judeophobia, that flower of the Ancien Régime, could only establish itself and flourish in autocratic societies or among the illiterate, where modernity had not yet taken hold. None but the primitive in outlook could give any credence to the myth of ritual murder, or really believe the blood libel – during the Damascus Affair of 1840, or the Beilis trial in Kiev in 1911, for instance – that Jews used the blood of Christian children or Capuchin monks to bake their unleavened bread . . .[8] And was it really a surprise that the Jewish Question came to a head in the poor and backward countries of Eastern Europe? Furious pogroms certainly worried Western Jews, but beyond such uneasiness, they became a source of optimism, confirming the vision of historical progress they held.

Full of promise, the cause of progress also imposed certain obligations, especially the need to change with the times. The Jews who *sinned against the future* by clinging to their communal past were no better than fear-mongering gentiles who believed Jews were the devil's children, or thought they poisoned wells. To combat such archaic behavior more effectively, the Jews worked hard at becoming *irreproachably modern men* themselves. Daily observances that would today signify only their cultural difference were for them signs of backwardness, and it became a point of honor to shed them. With historic eagerness, the Mosaic Law that had preserved them as a unique people and anti-Semitic myths were both subsumed under the category of prejudice or superstition. Their enemies' magical beliefs and their forefathers' nationalism were quickly dispatched; to the Israelites, those newborns of European civilization, this mythology, as well as this stubbornness, were equally contrary to the logic of history. What's past is past, petrified customs and sclerotic opinions alike. Progress demanded that Jewish uniqueness, along with old legends and their ancient fears that granted the people of Moses the powers of Satan, finally disappear.

In this they were doubly mistaken: anti-Semitism was not a relic, but a modern doctrine that had completely reworked its medieval and Christian themes. The new adepts at intolerance, moreover, were progressive militants, not retrograde bigots; they saved the brunt of their hatred for the most assimilated Jews. In Bessarabia, the Carpathians or other backward lands of Eastern Europe, no doubt, savages and unruly masses raged at traditional Jews. Yet in the heart of civilized Europe and at the very same moment, the learned, college-educated and socialists set on human betterment and its glorious future were showing that fanaticism and progress were not at all incompatible. And what was wrong with the Jews, as far as this intellectual and political avant-garde was concerned? Not their exclusivism or their immobility; not that they preferred their own law over the law of evolution, but that they were an anachronism, a scandal of history, a moment in time that refuses to die. The avant-garde blamed them for having infected the world, for foisting that shameful malady of capitalism upon it, and their own worship of money as well.

After emancipation, the "chosen people" broke their ancient ties and placed their bet on the universal. All energy thus had to be devoted to defending against the charge of separatism. Jews had worked so hard at successfully refuting this pernicious legend that a far more serious charge, being prepared at that very moment by the most sophisticated intellectuals, had gone unseen: the conspiracy myth. As ardent fighters for universal freedom of belief, the Israelites had cleared themselves of obstinately clinging to their identity. But even as they answered suspicions of their *stubbornness,* new adversaries arose to accuse them of attempting to *Jewify* society as a whole. Consider Gougenot des Mousseaux denouncing the Judaizing of Christian peoples and dastardly complots of the Alliance Israélite Universelle; consider Drumont, dripping with compassionate goodwill for the "avowed Jew," so easy to overlook because so easy to spot; consider this same Drumont already spouting Hitlerian curses against the "hidden Jew," that smooth and calculating animal, an elusive virtuoso of conspiracy and incognito master of sleaze, who by his very invisibility becomes the "dangerous animal par excellence," and "the most powerful trouble-making element the earth has ever produced."[9] Consider Marx correcting Hegel and claiming Jews are hardly the opinionated, unchanging people that the philosophy of history has always loved to represent: on the contrary, they are the most incendiary social issue of his day, "a timely and universal antisocial element," so powerful that "Christians have become Jewish."[10]

The episode of assimilation became a dialogue of the deaf: Jews defended themselves against a crime for which they were no longer being charged. Anti-Semites meanwhile took this Jewish blunder to be a bluff, a feint, and evidence of absolute guile. Here a long passage by the author of *Jewish France* must be cited, for there is no better example of historical irony attaining a tragic perfection. In 1931, two years before Hitler's accession to power, Bernanos still found it a source of amusement:

> For one hundred years the Jews have given us a running performance of *Deaf,* or *No Room at the Inn.* Israel enjoys toying with us in a conversation of fits and starts:
> "How is it that in several years almost the entire fortune of France has fallen into a few Jewish hands?"
> "What a terrible thing to say! You would let age-old prejudice keep us from worshipping the God of Jacob, prevent us from celebrating Yom Kippur and Pesach?"
> "You have descended on this unfortunate country like a cloud of locusts. You have subverted, bled and reduced it to poverty, you've orchestrated the most terrifying financial exploitation the world has ever known."
> "It's the festival of Sukkoth that bothers you? Sukkoth, that fine poetic festival of foliage! Come on, live in this century: religious liberty for all!"[11]

Won't the accused give straight answers? Don't they hear the complaints read against them? They must be trying not to hear, playing deaf: it's just the kind of devilish tactic that this deceitful, destructive, brilliant people would use. It's a well-known fact that deep guilt allows people to feign an innocence that's absolutely convincing. Such was the logic that would finally denounce the Israelites' pathetic naïveté as their crowning deception: the finishing touch of the tangled web they wove in darkness around the Western World.

The trial took place, the verdict was rendered, and for five years all of Europe was the site of punishment. The Jews were condemned to death. All Jews, regardless of age, sex, allegiance or way of life. In most European nations judges raged their denial that Jews were anything like one's fellow man, or even human beings. But the omnipotent magistrates disagreed about where Jews had gone wrong: some blamed the nation of Israel for not working hard enough to integrate. Others argued the opposite and found their efforts to be excessive, taking the Israelites' adaptability and appetite for modernity as proof of an unbridled will to power. At once unassimilable and too assimilated, Jews paid for these two contradictory accusations with a single death.

Then came the defeat of fascism and the purge of collaborators. Barbarity vanished from public discourse. Racial hatred was banned, though indistinct rumblings continued (and still do), quickly scrawled and written at night on cemetery walls or metro benches. But you no longer heard orchestrated incitements to murder, and the words *dirty Jew* and *kike,* which had reached their apotheosis during the war years, were suddenly heard no more. The word *Jew* itself became almost taboo: a swear word, a term for something obscene. Many no longer dared to use it, as if the word, too searingly direct, bore an insulting connotation. You were afraid that saying *Jew* would be a mark of questionable ties with collaborators or Nazis. You felt uneasy, were even repelled by a term that referred to a martyred community, the same term their executioners had used. Instead, you unctuously flaunted your use of the term *Israelites:* it was understood that this signified that you were free from all anti-Semitism, and that you actively sympathized with its victims. The word *Israelite* boomed in popularity; it's mere use was enough to amaze your friends and applaud your own forbearance and humanity. Those were the days. How sweet it was (not to mention economical): say a word and you had sided with the victims! A single word and you had been cleared, were transparently without blame! The same term which had previously referred only to assimilated Jews now came to signify the community as a whole. For the era of discrimination had passed, and the reign of euphemism had begun: it was no longer a question of separating good ones from the bad, but of brandishing and advertising your own goodwill toward Jews as a group.

And what did those concerned have to say? They kept silent. Such a careful, cautious change of vocabulary could give them little reason to hope. The sudden civility, the verbal tiptoeing, the faintly formal affectation of addressing the martyrs as *vous,* the perfunctory homage the conquered are accorded once their conquerors can no longer do harm: all this doubtlessly disturbed them. But they said nothing. Absorbed in their mourning and efforts to build a new life, they let the world buy back its virtue cheaply if it liked; they had bigger fish to fry, other nightmares and haunting fears. Much would be necessary for Jews to rise up openly and shed such reserve: the passage of time, the creation, strengthening and victories of the State of Israel, and finally the massive arrival of North Africa's Sephardim all played a part. Only then could Jews abandon their chic but safe kind of costume, the homogenized brand name that was *Israelite*.

Why this rejection? Because the attentive ear hears suave politeness and undertones of violence in the term *Israelite,* with both senses hardly perceptible. The voice of urbanity whispers: "Me, I don't use the term *Jew,* you know – I wish you only the best! Just look how virtuous I am!" Such exquisite courtesy blends in perfectly with demands to toe the line: "Don't act Jewish yourselves, don't show solidarity or flaunt your difference. And don't ever provide your detractors with ammunition for their calumny, for then you'll have failed to live up to the confidence I've placed in you, and in case of a crisis, I would be unable to help." *Israelite* is a doubly discredited term: for its pretentious display of humility and its dissimulated threat. With iron hand in velvet glove, those who use the term apparently wish to keep the Jews under surveillance and dictate their behavior, cost what it might. As if it were nothing. As if Jews owed the astonished and hostile reactions they received from their neighbors to nothing more than their own misanthropy. So it is that a single word allows the Holocaust to be whitewashed, and its meaning as an event to be hidden away.

Unfortunately enough for these affable tutors, *there are fewer and fewer Israelites in France*. A question of terminology? No: a judicial problem. Calling yourself an Israelite was a way of getting along, pleading assimilation, pleading you were like everyone else, and therefore not guilty; you played the game by agreeing to a perpetual examination, by graciously accepting being followed, noted and constantly scrutinized by dominant consciousness and its suspicious gaze. To call yourself a Jew, quite simply, is to affirm this: "We're neither guilty nor innocent: it's the idea of being on trial we reject forevermore. If some people think they can claim the right to run our lives, that's their business; we no longer accept our place in the defendant's chair. We've paid the price and now we know: according to the anti-Semites, we're wrong whatever we do. Wrong to be the Other, wrong to be just like everyone else. We will plead no longer, because our enemies have condemned us in advance, and because no higher court can decide upon collective identity for us, whether such authority calls itself 'France,' 'the State' or 'Man.' In proclaiming ourselves to be Jews instead of Israelites, we bring an era to a close, and declare that the time of surveillance and trials has passed."

Appendix

MARX, ANTI-SEMITISM AND "CLASS-STRUGGLEISM"

Marx an anti-Semite? Clearly he is, in *The Jewish Question,* a text from his youth that puts his considerable gifts in polemic and philosophy to work turning the flesh-and-blood Jew, his egotism and his business acumen into the emblem of bourgeois society. Marx's eminently *modern* anti-Semitism doesn't criticize the Jews for being historical holdovers, as the Hegelians did, but makes the opposite charge: the Jews are said to have *made* history, and achieved their greatest success while capitalist development was at its peak. From Hegel to Marx, the phobia remains just as intense – only the grievance has changed. And it becomes *more serious* yet. It is less distressing, all things considered, to be a people outside history, frozen in place and incapable of evolution, than to become the embodiment of everything unjust or abominable in the spirit of the age.

Marx would never return to this linkage between the Jews and money. In simplifying and deepening his reading of capitalism, he would demystify the noisy sphere of circulation, the "great secret" of surplus value, demystify both mercantile and industrial society alike, and get to the bottom of the ubiquity of money, the relations of production, exploitation and capital formation. Even after the equation of power with money has been broken, Marx the individual can certainly spew garbage at the Jews (which he does regularly in his correspondence). But his system will be free of all anti-Semitism.

This doesn't mean that Marxism is the best weapon for comprehending the hostility toward the people of Israel. Far more is required. From the point of view of so-called scientific socialism, an anti-Semite is very much like a traditional social-ist – someone fooled by the appearance of things. He mistakes the part for the whole, money for capital and Israelites for the bourgeoisie itself. Working-class anger is thereby displaced from those who are *truly guilty*. Hence the formulation of-fered by Bedel: anti-Semitism is the socialism of fools. It log-ically follows from this position that defending the Jews is a waste of revolutionary energy, distracting us from the *real vic-tims*. To a Marxist faithful to dogma, crying "Death to the Jews!" and accepting that Jews must fight alone are attitudes that share the same fetishistic point of view.

Take the Dreyfus affair. Who on the Left would make the most militant and activist claim for socialists to not get in-volved "in this bourgeois civil war"? It was Marx's followers, especially Guesde, who would lump "justice-mongers" and "patriotism-mongers" together, and calmly write:

> It might be time for us to remember that the goal of social-ism is not the liberation of a staff captain, but the freeing of the proletariat.

It was Jaurès who would finally rally socialists to the Drey-fusard cause; but in 1899, after Dreyfus's second trial, Karl Liebknecht and Rosa Luxemburg would express skepticism: to them it seemed impossible that a member of the ruling class could have been unjustly condemned.[12]

Five years later, April 1904, it's the massacre of Kishinev: forty-five Jews killed, hundreds of others wounded in the bloodiest pogrom in czarist history. The Jewish socialists of Poland and Russia, since 1897 an autonomous party (the Bund), draw this simple conclusion from the event: self-de-fense. Persecuted Jews must take their protection into their own hands. That's the theme of the speech that one of their leaders, Vladimir Medem, gives in Karlsruhe. And who arises to oppose him? Who is it whose implacable vehemence offers a refutation? A tall, thin, long-haired, yellow-shoed young man by the name of Leon Trotsky. Then an editor of *Iskra* and member of the circle in the process of forming, with Lenin's guidance, Bolshevik doctrine, Trotsky develops the strict version of "class-struggleism." To Medem's appeal for self-defense, Trotsky replies that the fight against anti-Semitism cannot be *singled out,* must not even be considered a separate topic for discussion by the masses. The level of general consciousness must be raised; only then will anti-Semitism disappear.[13]

Caught between the bourgeoisie and the proletariat, incidental victims of exploitation or substitute targets for the exploited, the Jewish people can lay claim to only a peripheral role in the dynamic of history. Marxists relegated these subalterns of oppression to the cheap seats.

They will never admit that the Jews might be treated as a full-fledged enemy by a capitalist regime. And this includes Nazism. To do so would be a sacrilegious challenge to the logic of class. This is why even in May 1942, the underground newspaper *Humanité* would insist on distinguishing between that collaborator Rothschild and impoverished, persecuted Jews, and would treat deportations based on race and the general requisition of workers as if they were the same thing.

On the contrary: when did Marxists suddenly become so interested in the Jews of Western Europe? Only when the notion of a universal class fell into crisis, and the Marxist vision of history as well.[14]

5
The Ostentation of Nothingness

"Here, look at me, over here!" People are all face. Everybody's too much. . . . We're all constantly showing off, even when we're alone, when no one's looking. We've all gone public, inside and out. We keep enhancing our image. – Botho Strauss

French Jews are no longer ashamed of their name. They shout it from the rooftops, unlike the past when it was confided in hushed whispers, those days when their religion was scarcely acknowledged and had to be kept under wraps. They are no longer Israelites, but henceforth Jews, recovering from a constant, obsessive fear of disappointing. Knights without fear and without reproach, these little Bayards of Jewishness confront the eyes of the majority with calm self-assurance: as themselves, without makeup. Nothing if not eager students, Israelites would anxiously ask: "Did I get it right?" Then it was always back to the drawing board: either because they hadn't done enough to earn the love of their adoptive mother France – lending credence to the idea that they constituted a nation within a nation – or because they'd done too much, been so eager to please that they'd given clumsy hints of a background they sought to suppress. The days of the double bind were over. After having kept their essential being at arm's length for so long, French Jews now savor the pleasures of difference recaptured.

An unlikely sort of difference, this flaunting of a void: for what do I affirm when I say: "I am a Jew"? I de-alienate myself, if you will, from imposed roles – Citizen, Man, the Frenchman from France – I escape the servitude that foreign powers sought to impose. But I find no lasting comfort in such liberty, for my inner life is empty. Freed from enchantment and henceforth immune to assimilation's charms, I emphatically claim the right to be myself, to be a self that is nothing, nothing but an unending obsession and imaginary tale. With illusions of patriotism or the grand delusion of universalism no longer standing between me and my Jewish truth, the latter seems to vanish into thin air.

There was once a rabbi who ran feverishly through the streets of the Prague ghetto: "I have an answer," he said, "I have an answer . . . Who has a question?" His successor today paces the cities of the West; he no longer wears a caftan or beard, and no one pays any attention to his distress: "I am different," he says, "I am different . . . Who can assure me it's true?"

SOCIETY IN A THOUSAND PIECES
Those assimilated, those shirkers, those cowards we no longer wish to be: their Jewishness showed in spite of themselves. The less they were heard from, the more their silence began to seem disturbing or strange. Those simian smiles, that submissive posture were just a ruse of war. If they expressed their hopes for tranquility, for peace, to fade into the background, it was seen as evidence of their tentacular presence, a telltale sign of their secret government. Jewish attempts at assimilation came to resemble the useless struggles of a man running fast, hoping to leave his shadow behind. No sooner had the strict and singular regimen of Jewish life come to an end than

did the Jew become a *character*: a fateful sort of heredity, special temperament, a personality, a set of types. With the death of overt Jewish difference, Jewishness leapt into the breach and carried the flag. Neither religion nor a daily routine, Jewishness was an individual essence that underlay every aspect of behavior. As a way of comporting oneself that was both insidious and totalitarian, it was a kind of instinct anchored in the deepest recesses of the self, where one's psychological secrets could be read. The Jew no longer different from other men? Looks the same, has the same sober dress, the same faddish tastes and public behavior? Did he willingly place himself under the same temporal scheme as others, agree to follow the same daily routine as everyone else? Don't believe it for a minute! Jewishness arose precisely in order to provoke such a *blackout,* and racism just in time to carry on the work that the clarity of segregation had formerly achieved. Anti-Semitism turned racist only on the fateful day when, as a consequence of Emancipation, you could no longer pick Jews out of a crowd at first glance.

Since the Jews – those revolting mimics – were no longer distinguishable by any particular trait, they were graced with a distinct mentality. Science was charged with succeeding where the gaze had failed, asked to make sure that the adversary remained foreign, to stigmatize the nation of Israel by enclosing it within a Jewish reality. Fear and resentment were the roots of the determinism that made Rothschild a business genius, Dreyfus a traitor, and considered every Jew to be a cross between the two. Racial hatred and its blind rage were essentially the Jews' punishment for no longer placing their difference on display. As if fatal instinct alone could make them expiate the indeterminate status they'd suddenly assumed. The Israelites said they were just like everyone else, an audacious presumption they would pay for with an alterity that was radical, despotic, infinite. Until then the Jews had

83

been only a variety – albeit a tough one – of infidel; they were about to become a subspecies in the great bestiary of mankind.

It was an ironic fate for those dedicated Frenchmen to be treated as aliens, plutocrats, men whose spirits were possessed by the evils of barbarian rites. Contemporary Jews don't have their patience; they assert their identity, however much it displeases those who are obsessed with the State or nostalgic for an essentially Christian France. As a result, yesterday's unwilling draftees to assimilation are today succeeded by Jews who are assimilated *in spite of themselves*. The Gallic Jews, our ancestors, won only precarious victories against exclusion. Temporary and revocable, their Frenchness could be called into question at the first sign of scandal; the slightest crisis sufficed to repatriate them to the Jewish condition of their birth. Not us: we've exposed the terror and lies of assimilation for what they are. We no longer believe the pretty promises. French and immigrant Jews are reconciled in self-affirmation, and share the same keen insight – the time for patriotic lyricism and emotional pleas for national unity has passed. Yet our disillusioned skepticism is itself illusory; basically, we denounce assimilation as a trap, now that on the whole it's no longer forced upon us, and blind ourselves to how much like everyone else we've already become. We reject the fool's errand that yesterday's Israelites willingly undertook. We've every reason to congratulate ourselves for our staunchness and renewed unity as a group.

But doesn't this scant the paradox of a modernity in which people holding quite different beliefs act in an increasingly identical fashion? That is: at the very moment that we reject assimilationist thinking, we're helpless to resist the standardization of the self. Our exultant and theatrical revolt confuses yesterday's nationalist France with the open society of "weak ideological integration" we belong to today (Annie Kriegel).

By saying an emphatic "NO!" to the homogenization of social identity, we act as if an aggressive, closely knit nation were rising to confront us, setting draconian limits on our rights as citizens. But is integration still a contract, a dialogue between two living communities, or already under way as a *process* that no longer requires individual consent? Which epoch is really our own? The days of France indivisible, or the era when the great collective entities are dissolved?

Knowing the names of flowers and the thirty-six thousand kinds of cheese. Being a wine expert and a specialist in dishes served in sauce. Taking personal interest in the infinite subtleties of an inexplicable orthography. Never contaminating your vocabulary with foreign words. Creating a barricade of subjunctives, fortifying your speech with rules and grammatical exceptions as so many protections against the invader. Having intimate knowledge of the masterpieces of our literary heritage. Singing the glory of Du Guesclin or of Jean Bart. Getting goose bumps at the memory of the coronation at Reims, and always feeling the same emotion when reading the account of the festival of the Federation. Being willing to give your life for your country on a moment's notice. Until quite recently, this is what it meant to be French. And these were the criteria used to measure the extent to which Jews had really become part of France. Today, the magnetism no longer holds. Deprived of its former attraction, the paradigm fractures and falls apart. And not just for Jews. The disaffection has become general: the French on the whole are distancing themselves from any such collective enthusiasm. No longer finding commonality in their territorial identity, they imperceptibly cease dramatizing France.

And so, along with the Jewish minority, the bulk of the populace is abandoning the majoritarian model that hails from the days of assimilation. Nation, Republic – these words have the scent of the past. From the world of exotica to the flea market, from retro to métro, the fascination is gone: they're strictly a source of amusement, their myth reduced to folklore. For want of tender loving care, two Frances are perishing together, dying from indifference: garden France, in which each citizen was a native plant, or better still, a tree rooted in its soil, whence it drew its truth and creative energy like sap in the spring, and the France of the Republic, which made Marianne a mistress to all who were French and '89 their date of birth. Not that everyone became tired of democracy or longed for the monarchy's return. But why should anyone believe in the Republic? Do we have faith in the air we breath? This regime can do without devotion and heroism: it's too established to retain a romantic air, and its undeniable presence makes the grand passions it once stirred seem passé. Marianne's lovers have become few because she no longer has enemies. In similar fashion, nationalist zeal has been replaced by detachment. Gone are the Krauts who helped sustain a mystical sense of place and regionalism's religious love. We have lost the hereditary enemies who sacralize the land on which we live. "The fatherland in danger!"– a meaningless expression. There can be no fatherland, no national consciousness without a definable menace, only an atomized world, a society scattered into countless little groups of individuals instead.

It is not peace per se that put an end to grand feelings of soldierly solidarity, and to the bellicose joy of ancient epic, but *the modern image of war*. The peril awaiting us is not the stuff of which such religion or mythology can be built. No geographic boundary can stand up to the nuclear threat. Today, impending conflict diminishes what it gave rise to in the past: a world divided into camps of the native-born and the foreign, and exacerbated feelings of national identity. Current technology makes the tool more important than the actors, as technical means erase borders and antagonisms. We no longer experience war as a gamelike confrontation or battle, but as a tragic

86

kind of planetary fate. On one side stands the instrument of death, and on the other, the people, its victims regardless of the passport we hold. The chief deterrent effect of strategic weapons is their discouragement of patriotic ardor. With the bomb, war's violence has reached adulthood and left individual aggressivity behind. Nuclear weapons have thus succeeded where several centuries of humanism have failed: by *disarming* nationalism, they have forcibly removed modern man from his region's hypnotic hold.

Always the newcomers, Jews didn't love humus, or the soil, or the exaltation of forests. They understandably mistrusted a pastoral lyricism and nationalist impulse invoked to shut them out. When their compatriots offered excessively eloquent apostrophes to the wisdom of the woods and the forests' peace, they knew an anti-Jewish campaign couldn't be far behind. And so they played one France against the other: Danton against Maurras, and the universalist principles of the Revolution against the intuitionist dogma of cultural roots. While several European countries fell under the hegemony of a biological nationalism, French Israelites lived in a Janus-faced country that gave them the right to choose whatever sort of patriotism suited them best. They could condemn passionate regional attachments in the name of an attachment to reason, which was just as deep. If mystical, organic or racial France didn't want them, they'd belong to the France of the Jacobins, successfully integrate into society by those alternate, sometimes marginal but perfectly acceptable ideological routes: freedom of thought, love of the Republic or socialism.

Once again I note how much the Jewish idea, at least for Jews of the time, was a natural fit with the spirit of the Revolution, and the ease, the kind of pre-established harmony with which they adopted its dogmas, by which so many Frenchmen were repelled.[1]

87

Whether children of immigrants or French by stock, most Jews reject such conduct. To be an impeccable patriot is worthless, they say, since love of France will never abolish anti-Semitism. And even if it could, the forced sacrifice of uniqueness to achieve social standing is unacceptable. Haunted by recent history and its phantoms, Jews turn their situation into a Don Quixote routine. Instead of opposing the Jacobin ideal with an integral nationalism, in the tradition of earlier generations, they repudiate both models at once. It's a legitimate revolt, but an anachronistic one, for it rejects an important fact: both of these Frances are in decline. Now a banal and disenchanted space, the fatherland is no longer a cause to die for, and members of the majority culture are died-in-the-wool nationalists no more.

With the rise of particularism comes the twilight of citizenship as an ideal. The most common tack to take in a society bereft of common beliefs and collective heroism is to turn inward, value the self before all else and, most importantly, to carve out your individual niche. Conformity today finds its point of departure in a rejection of any common ground, of any site where French society could pause and face its own reflection. In other words, what characterizes the average Frenchman is not, as blind elitism would have it, the obsession with keeping up with Pierre, but the cultivation of the self. You can only belong in this narcissistic society by becoming an individual and distinguishing yourself from the group. Rebellion becomes the normative gesture, and securing one's difference is the dominant social impulse – the herd instinct in its modern form.

Let's not kid ourselves. France has not even scratched the surface where the civilities of racial integration or cosmopolitanism are concerned. Though militarism and the battle cries of nationalism are held in contempt, individuals continue to judge one another – to test, to join, to exclude – in a frantic, neverending quest. Such classificatory work, however, will never produce a totalizing, binary opposition that will separate inside from outside once and for all. The more our world becomes fragmented, the more reasons for exclusion there are. Aesthetic and sartorial racism, regional xenophobia, partition by language, segregation by age, race, social class and lifestyle: all these interwoven distrusts are gradually replacing simple discrimination by the Frenchman against his Other.

As a Jewish individual, I face an out-of-joint social landscape that the national idea no longer sets right. Society's paradigms are multiple, shifting and contradictory. I experience acceptance, then rejection, and come to know both situations: the pleasure of inclusion as well as ostracism's bitter rage. Yet the question of whether I show a properly unconditional love of France decreases in importance as the concept of the Fatherland becomes more and more abstract and loosens its grasp; a nationalism in decline can't be held responsible for my lack of complete social inclusion, or for the frosty reception I sometimes receive.

To tell the story of the formative years of a Jew born around 1950 of immigrant parents, a new genre would have to be forged: the novel of "dis-apprenticeship." The child enters the world with the wisdom of a patriarch. Disillusioned, wary and untrusting, without any period of innocence, he knows – or thinks he knows – that he is but a tenant in France, a barely tolerated visitor, and that the country of the Rights of Man is a house divided, with an invisible line separating the owner from the guests.

Yet the Jewish child grows up in a state of increasing confusion. Wisdom gradually turns to perplexity, and indecision nibbles away at the feeling of insight he held at the start. His own community, and the House of Israel to which he belongs – where are they actually to be found? Apart from the family, the Jewish community is a fiction that exists only in the rhetoric of its promoters. Of course there are institutions, a press, schools, important figures, charitable works; but like most of his peers, he lives beyond this network and its reach. As a Jew he is spokesman for an abstract "us," counsel to a collectivity without any collective existence.

Second surprise: the Other side, as a group, is no more unified than is his native tribe. The world before him bears no resemblance to the picture his disillusioned certainties had drawn. The pessimistic child is replaced by an adolescent, not thrilled or blessed but *disoriented*. His first realization: there's more than one kind of goy. The France he thought he knew so well is a state without an identity. Growing up for this young Jew means losing his bearings. He who was solemnly ready to choose between faith and rejecting his people confronts the absolute vanity these alternatives imply. Assimilation is not the rite of passage he had come to expect. No odyssey of initiation will take place. There's nothing to boast about, for he's had to do away with any such voyage. Both his point of embarkation and the land of his homecoming – his community's Jewishness, and France as one nation indivisible – have disappeared from the map. If they can be found, it's only as remnants. The heir to a divided world acclimatizes himself slowly to a new social geography.

Two representations will finally impose themselves on him: one depicts a *fragmented* society in pieces, where the old division between "them" and "us" is replaced by a proliferation of social castes, hierarchies and incompatible universes; the other representation portrays an increasingly *uniform* society, where the same schedule, habits and demands of work and leisure, the same television, the same secular public schools shape both Jew and goy.

In the past there were many Jews who abandoned their community without actually taking up residence in another. They no longer inhabited the Jewish world, and the dominant society was hesitant to accept them. Such Jews were hybrid beings, recognizable members of neither of the species from which they had been produced. As failed deserters, men from nowhere, they were suspended in the anguish that comes of living in an in-between kind of world, "with their posterior legs still glued to their father's Jewishness, and with their waving anterior legs they found no new ground."[2] The postwar Jewish child has long believed these same words could express the essence of his destiny. But this will be the last stage of his "dis-apprenticeship," and he will have to mourn his fate. Whatever else may be the case, he is not the pathetic victim of a double exclusion. His integration was carried out gently, under anesthesia, in a process he was powerless to choose. For in the absence of cultural values he could freely reject or make his own, there is still the culture of everyday life – industrious, hedonistic, televisual and intellectual – denying him, like everyone else, any privileged position outside its grasp.

FROM THE MODEL JEW TO THE JEWISH MODEL

Alienation: the magic word we use to account for the pathogenic effects of modern life. You don't feel good about yourself? You feel inadequate or worried, are subject to fits of depression or long bouts of black despair? The diagnosis is unmistakable, automatic: you're alienated, manifest every symptom of the alienated individual, and all your problems can come only from this addiction that you can't kick. The internalized Other: that's the root of the problem (the Other as generic figure, the Father, the Mother, the System or Society fit the bill just as well). In each case, the plenitude of the self is inaccessible to those who are vulnerable or easily influenced, remain under the sway of external forces, and are *not yet individual enough*. Modern morality asks each of us to perform a kind of inner housecleaning. Rediscovering oneself has come to resemble a kind of eviction for undesirable renters who take up too much space. And even more so when they're members of the family. The idea is to face the world as your own person, to achieve full self-presence at the moment when the word *I* is pronounced. It's a seductive process, turning individual existence into a theater and a wager at once. Yet perhaps we're alienated, more than anything, by the idea of alienation itself. The noisy neuroses of those no longer in touch with themselves are a disguise, hiding the suffering or lassitude that come with the realization that they are themselves and nothing more.

Just look around and you'll see the envy some people harbor for the Jewish condition. I've even come across unhappy Christians, surprising goyim, who are so fascinated with the longevity and unparalleled destiny of the Jewish people that they dream of becoming Jews. That's right: French Catholics, people of the land, "one of us," with a house in the Creuse, a Grandmother in the Poitou, Auvergnat cousins, who are jealous of the Jews! Who envy their collective memory, their intense sense of belonging and the immutable bonds that bind them to a unique history and living community; who envy the inherent transcendence that makes them more than mere individuals, that quality of having something extra, in a word, that shatters the repetition of me-me-me, and removes them from the stagnation of an exclusively personal existence. To be Jewish: or, the chance to escape yourself.

But let's not blow the situation out of proportion. The world's not topsy-turvy, and there aren't many "true-blue" Frenchmen casting furtive glances Judaism's way or thinking that living with minority status would be a lucky turn of fate. Nor is it clear, despite the security they enjoy, that Jews today have more friends than in the past. In crises, on the contrary, people's tongues are suddenly set free, ancient inhibitions are broken and the persistence of anti-Semitism brutally shines forth.[3]

One thing is certain: in a few short years, philo-Semitism has put on a new face, acquired a new governing principle and changed its nature. "Jews are human beings like the rest of us." Since the Age of Enlightenment, such has been the position taken by generous souls. Man had worth because he was a man, regardless of ancillary traits such as nationality or religion. Today we are much more tempted to say: "It's Jewishness that keeps this individual from being reduced to himself." The obstacle to desire becomes his cause; the secondary trait is elevated to a privilege. Man as empty subject, so to speak, is voided in favor of his attributes. Humanist tolerance cedes its place to a completely new feeling comprised of admiration and nostalgia.

Old-fashioned Judeophiles were kindly old pedagogues and overindulgent fathers. With never a harsh word and limitless patience, they knew no discouragement, they bolstered confidence, loving their students and defending them passionately against those who would have excluded them from class. For they knew that the Jews, despite their tardiness as a group, would eventually make excellent Frenchmen, model citizens and irreproachable men. These were philanthropists who appreciated Jews not for what they were but for the perfect peers they were to become. They promised to bring out their human essence, gambled on the risky potential of these newcomers to transform themselves into something other than what they were. Nothing that was foreign was inhuman for these tireless liberals. There was no kind of difference, however forbidding, that they didn't hope finally to neutralize and reduce.

Today's philo-Semites have given up on teaching and abandoned any pretense of mastery. Paternalism was finished when Jews acceded to the dignity of models. There's nothing left to teach the sons of Abraham: there they are, exemplifying the very values that anti-Semitic prejudice claimed they would absolutely resist. Jews now provide occasion for celebrating a world and its principles that they were accused, not long ago, of wanting to destroy. French, Catholic, Western: there are people for whom these designations no longer mean a thing. Their drawing power has been nullified, and their power to evoke is nonexistent. Not even negative qualities, they're abstract data, diaphanous attributes of individuals who would never use them to describe who they are. These sullen members of the majority culture have the white bread blues, feel a woeful lack of belonging – the deep depression that comes of living without a native land.

To people such as these prisoners of the egosphere, Jews seem blessed by history: part of their being is not of the self but transcends it, partakes of a vaster group and greater temporal scheme. A patrimony, a faith and a spiritual dimension is theirs, with a role in the course of human events that cannot be summarized by personal anecdote alone. Founded on law, their existence is protected against the vague terrors of contingency. In an era of humdrum lives, Jewishness seemingly provides an enviable reason to live. The image of the Jew is undergoing a kind of reversal of fortune: now he is the one who has roots, and it's the French philo-Semite, that poor wandering goy, who sees himself as deracinated and stateless, a man without qualities.

May '68: a time of verbal terrorism and exuberant life. An age of wooden rhetoric and passionate togetherness, of overheated politics and a discovery of communication. All of which brings the actors of that vanished era to speak derisively as well as affectionately of May and its legacy. Their past is first an object of irony, then of nostalgia, a time of weakness when the wildest dogma flourished, and a powerful time when a beautiful collective epic was forged. Perhaps this is the source of our new perspective on minorities as a whole and Jews in particular. In a world deprived of majestic causes and grand reasons to live, the privilege of historical consistency seems reserved to them alone.

For us Jews, this was quite a promotion. To see our identity not only recognized but given strokes, even envied by some, makes us blush like a young girl showered with flowers by an eager suitor. Other times it makes our heads spin, and we play the coquette. We become the person they describe. Why fight it? We succumb voluptuously to the character they believe they uncover in us: anxious, tortured, wary, chosen by History and cursed among men. A painful fever overtakes us; a sort of metaphysical transport makes our existence more intense. However improbable and tenuous it may have been previously, our Jewishness turns delectably deep. Our relationship with mortality and with Mother is Jewish, and it's Jewish insomnia we suffer, replete with feelings of guilt that attack in the night; our vital need for books is Jewish as well, so too our need for Jewish concepts and for living and breathing the written word. And of course it almost goes without saying: there's our Jewish sense of humor, full of tenderness or despair. There's nothing opaque, absurd or ordinary in our reactions anymore. Now it's the marvelously distinct clarity of being different: the pleasure of seeing ourselves as the House of Israel's legitimate child.

But the feeling of intoxication doesn't last. *Sober*, we lose the illusion that we represent our people and its culture in each and every situation. The identity we claimed as rightful owners is gone. Do these elaborate affectations have any real basis? On behalf of what do we so transparently wrap ourselves in mystery, taking on a conspiratorial aura, we who have an empty secret as our only common bond? The game of "Who am I?" will be a short one, for the Jewish content of our lives isn't enough to rub two sticks together. Here we are, elevated to the status of historical models, but after the bleaching we've undergone, there's not much left to justify our spectacular rise.

For this "we" has no real provenance. It represents not the Jews of France in their entirety, but the majority of lost and isolated souls who, like me, harbor the impotent dream of assimilating back into their original culture. This "we" is comprised of individuals who feel Jewish and who, tired of pure affectivity, would like to break the bounds of the self-engendered pathos in which their Jewishness has been enclosed, of people just like everyone else, trying to convince themselves that they're somehow different from the norm. They're the children and grandchildren of immigrants, handed proud difference as a legacy in trust; they can realize it only through the means they possess: the vaguest reminiscences, a moribund symbolic system and a language that lies in shreds. These are creatures, finally, who have only their imagination to resist the herd. So they don't resist. And to hide their capitulation, they advertise their origin, shout it from the rooftops and become dizzy from the clamor they make. They flaunt their Jewishness, thinking that audacity of gesture can compensate for the irreality it displays. They can certainly proclaim their right to be different, but the only content they're able to give this otherness is the lively or vehement emphasis with which their affirmation is made.

A Jew within, a man without: this, you will recall, was the slogan of the first assimilation. Without always admitting it to ourselves, we practice the same principle in reverse: we're Jews without, for our friends, for the public, for the outside world, while within, in the intimacy of our daily lives, we're just like everybody else, followers of the same styles and prey to the same fascinations, without any cultural specificity all our own.

That's why there are so many Jewish romantics these days. They run about repeating it everywhere: "I'm a Jew," waxing euphoric over their own sincerity. This is Judaism reduced to self-enunciation, completely exhausted by its own discourse. It's not religious affiliation that's brought to the fore, but a character worthy of prestige. The need to stand out is clearly perceptible beneath the surface of collective affirmation. The word *Jew* is worn like a brooch on a dark gray suit: a tiny detail that tears you away from everyday sorrows and makes you stand out.

To have done with this decorative Judaism, some young Jews rediscover the austere charms of tradition. Sometimes scrupulously and sometimes casually, they draw on the immense heritage of ritual gestures that orthodoxy has bequeathed. They throw themselves into the joys of observance, and get a taste for those demanding practices that their family often made it a duty *not* to impose on them: keeping the sabbath and the major holidays of the Jewish year. Such neo-archaic return to tradition sometimes goes so far as keeping kosher, an infinitely detailed, exacting and rigid dietary code. The bigotry of the younger generation, you say? One symptom among a thousand of the sacred's resurgence in a hostile world where skepticism has lost its hold? Perhaps. But many of the newly observant shamelessly dissociate ritual from belief. Nothing mystical in their enthusiastic loyalty. With lives ruled by schedule, they reinvented ritual obligation and its customs. With whatever means were available. As dilettantes. As tinkerers. And this imperious need for constraints is no profession of faith, but a claim to belonging.

What's correctly described here as religious renewal derives only from those aspects of the movement that go beyond the intimist conception of the religious individual. It's a renewal dependent on worn procedures and their anachronistic rules, and on those daily prescriptions that had already marked Judaism as out of date in the eyes of Enlightenment philosophes. Jewish spirituality paradoxically owes its modernity to legalism, which makes it possible to attach oneself concretely to a nation without land. Does God exist? Whatever the case, you needn't have met him to justify your existence on legal grounds. The great merit of this tradition (or at least its considerable contemporary value) is to turn the question away from divinity and not make it into a prerequisite. Faith is secondary, for the rediscovery of ritual is certainly the expression of a bond, but one that links Jews with themselves (and with their dead) rather than with the Eternal.

Such is the venture of these practicing agnostics, and such is the deep desire behind their return to outmoded exercises of faith. It's not to reduce *Jewish* to simply an adjectival piece of statuary, but to make Jewishness something other than a title, an emblem, or a flamboyant form of ignominy; to transform a declaration of identity into a way of life; to substitute an active cultural experience for the coquettish presentation of self. God for them is neither present nor hidden: he is *optional*.

Perhaps the synagogue finds this need for observance pleasing in spite of the atheism it contains. Perhaps the spirits of the consistory and the Jewish establishment are roused to see so many young Jews returning to the fold who previously slumbered in self-forgetfulness, or whom the apocalyptic discourses of leftism had led astray. It's no time, however, to break out the bunting and flags. For what does this sudden passion for the law mean if not that in Europe (outside showing solidarity with the State of Israel), religion constitutes the sole expression of Jewish life. There's no longer any choice: it's ritual or nothing, repetition or disappearance, the tradition – with or without God – or the void. For the assassination of Yiddish killed not just a language but a cultural universe, a way of being in the world that is Jewish without being automatically religious. No one has the right to confine Judaism to the Bible or the Talmud. Mourning must not be dressed up as a triumph. We must not submit to the verdict of facts. Is there really any worse kind of resignation than the one that turns history into a historical tribunal? If all roads now seem to lead to the Ten Commandments, it's because violence, not long ago, was used to prohibit or to erase other itineraries of Jewish life.

The rites that we perpetuate with the timidity of novices and the clumsiness of amateurs are neither the heart nor the whole of Judaism: they are the remains. The last chance for a people whose other cultures have been killed or turned to folklore. The single and fragile chance that has been given us to move beyond dreaming and to not be imaginary Jews.

6

The Different States of the Child Prodigy's Soul

I kept seeing myself coming back to New Jersey and saying to my family, "I met a marvelous young woman while I was up in New England. I love her and she loves me. We are going to be married." "Married? But so fast? Nathan, is she Jewish?" "Yes, she is." "But who is she?" "Anne Frank." – Philip Roth

Upon learning that he had been sentenced to life in exile for high treason and espionage, Alfred Dreyfus collapses into his brother's arms: "Mathieu, Mathieu, am I under some kind of curse? What fatality pursues me?"[1]

By chance during a nighttime stroll, the hero of *The Snake's Egg* sees his name on the sign of a Jewish store: Rosenberg. In wild and impotent rage he throws a rock through his eponymous window, as if to conjure up an image of his own destiny. We're in Berlin, in 1923.

Two decades later: how many people treated as prey, under threat of raids or being denounced to the police, imprisoned in camps or condemned to the slow death of the ghettos, how many victims of a stereotypic face or last name, how many wearers of the yellow star must have experienced an almost vertiginous rage at being born Jews! Logic demanded that the lion's share of blame be placed on the regime that organized genocide and on those societies whose apathy or complacency made the Nazis' gigantic venture possible. But such rational resistance was no defense against the certainty of death. Another feeling followed in its wake, a silent, mad indictment of God, of Chance, of the Universe and of Providence. "Why me? Why do I, without any prior consultation, have to be a member of a sacrificed people. Why, in addition to the burden of being human, must I carry the weight of the Jewish condition as well? What have I done to deserve a place among the living dead?" In times of persecution, there is surely not a single Jew, no matter how proud of Israel, who has not cursed his Jewishness to heaven.

Our generation, spared the tragic (and which calls itself "lost," in antiphrasis no doubt), has never known the incomprehensible distress that gives rise to the cry "Why me?" We've had our share of anger and feeling sick and tired, and have something to add when the difficulty of being Jewish is discussed. But we've overestimated its seriousness. Our generation's most gifted and impetuous representatives are wrong when they occasionally use the years of darkness to characterize their own. Our mounting cries, our pouting and our foot-stamping never directed themselves against transcendence, nor even took society as their target. For all our metaphysical pretensions, the family was the sole object of our resentment during an adolescence without end.

By broadcasting my wish to be a Jew, and my uneasiness at being such a poor one, I delayed making a more delicate confession. In pious silence, I overlooked those moments of weakness when – there's no other way to say it – I was sick and tired of being Jewish. Disgusted . . . saturated . . . stuffed to the gills with it . . . I'd had enough, been worn out from repetition, was numbed by hackneyed clichés about our peerless destiny, bludgeoned with the constant refrain about a people whom no one loved. The prize goose was asking for mercy – not God's, or the system's, but from those feeders, my parents and their perpetual Jewish obsession. Obsession is the word. I was spared no instruction, strictures, no obligatory practice. Under the guise of spiritual nourishment, I absorbed only a droning fixation on my identity. I was the daily recipient of a qualifier repeated until I was dazed. And so, sometimes the temptation was just too much. Was it the seriousness I couldn't stand anymore? Or was it the drivel? I gave in, in any case, to the temptations of scandal, and responded to this Jewish litany by taking an opposite course. It wasn't just a matter of my taste for the comic or my spirit of contradiction. Something more serious was at stake. For me it was a question of being myself, and since you can strike a pose well only while opposing something else, the only way to achieve autonomy in my thoroughly Jewish world was to play the absolute goy. After all, I was taught from an early age to take pride in being a minority, by my parents themselves. Didn't they constantly remind me of *our* solitude and *our* curse, and that for all our misery and glory, our number was few? I liked that: I was so enamored of my misfortune that it was hard for me to endure those rare moments among Jews when I was like everyone else. Playing the goy, I felt a bit like the Jew of the family. . .

They talked about Israel every time they listened to the news; I responded with Vietnam, imperialist crimes and the culpability of all pro-Americans. If they brought up the question of anti-Semitism in France, I immediately interrupted by affirming that there were indeed no Jewish garbage collectors, and that today, immigrant workers were the only victims of racism. In short, I de-Judaized myself at home – that is, at the table – for the very same reasons that drove me in public – that is, at school – to proclaim my Jewish identity: to feel like I really existed and transcend the commonplace, to not be the interchangeable spokesperson for the majority view. I had but a single objective – difference – but living in two universes with contradictory rules, I had to split myself in two to realize my plan. Wanting so much to be the Other, I was no longer anything at all, just a messenger, a go-between who riled his parents with arguments he heard in school and confronted his schoolmates with the compassionate speeches his parents had bequeathed.

This split is rather common; it's even natural for adolescents to feel divided between their family's values and their friends' view of the world. But this classic setup presents the Jewish child with a difficulty that's unique. Because it lacks a precise content, his Jewishness has no stable bounds. There's no dividing line in the Jewish family separating principles from sentiment. Everything is love, and everything, at the same time, is Jewishness. The confusion is a constant source of our finest neuroses and responsible for our most amazing character: the Jewish Mother. This mother, to be precise, is no more possessive, abusive or passionate than any other. She can't claim the distinction of being the most affectionate. What makes her a special case is not the kind of bond linking her to her progeny but rather the openness with which this attachment is expressed. Every mother is nostalgic for the paradise of harmonious unity in which, for two or three years of unadulterated happiness, she and her infant once lived. Every mother experiences the gradual independence of the child she has carried as a kind of abandonment. But in general, Maternal Love is there, watchful and self-policing: repressing, concealing, censuring and sublimating any expression that bears too close a resemblance to the needs of passionate love. The traditional mother pitilessly weeds out such emotions, sacrificing the most excessive ones to preserve her sacred self-image. And so she comes to know all love's trials – jealousy, abandonment, loneliness – without even being able to take pleasure in the bitter consolation of words. She suffers doubly, from an unrequited passion and from self-imposed censorship. Society demands that she disappear and keep quiet too. Except for commonplace exchanges, complaining is forbidden her, for verbal compensation isn't written into the rules. That's why your mother is silent. Mum's the word and bite your lip: she relegates to the obscurity of the unspoken all the spite, the violence, every drive that blatantly contradicts the celestial ideal of the mother our civilization has come to produce.

The Jewish mother doesn't take such precautions. She'd rather be the talkative type. Alienated from her children? She certainly is, but absolutely free in voicing her dependence. What's immediately striking about her, making her unique, is the innocence of her affection, the complete serenity with which this impenitent Jocasta allows herself to fall in love with her little ones. Without fuss. Shamelessly, without shunning the melodramatic in the least. Not that she's excused as a kind of exception or through ethnic prerogative from the strict prohibitions placed on maternal love. But this spontaneous, this expansive, this extremist mother has an alternative at her disposal that's denied other women, reduced for the most part to self-deception and denial. The ultimate weapon: *displacement*. Subject to infinite variations, the Jewish mother, in fact, knows how to make her desires heard. It's enough to give her a unique moral stance, to define her Jewishness. With it, a fit of jealousy is easily turned into a demand that you keep the faith. The "Don't leave me," the "Be mine" of maternal desire becomes "Don't forget your origins," and the incalculable nuance tosses prohibition aside, renders possessiveness legitimate. The sacred mission with which the mother feels herself invested – to perpetuate the Jewish people – is what allows her to complain. For then everything is reversed: it's no longer mother's love that's at fault, but the indifference of her beloved. In Christian society, the Jewish family and Jewish nation are two indistinguishable structures: leaving one in any way means deserting the other. That's why the Jewish mother will soon disappear from the State of Israel. The Diaspora is the world she prefers. There alone can the independence of her child be translated into a kind of treason. It's the goys, in short, who have made the Jewish mother's privileged expressiveness and good conscience possible. Without them, she'd have no right to complain, and would have to return to the silent unhappiness of the muzzled masses of other mamas.

And now, think of Portnoy and his odd torments.[2] Are you really surprised at his appetite for provoking conflict, or at his constant, unwavering desire for non-Jewish women? Do you really think it's strange that he has what's almost a need, when he loves, to enrage his family? Each neurosis produces another. The mother defends herself from self-criticism by defining her desire as Jewish, while Portnoy, in response, defends himself against a serious charge – incest – by removing everything Jewish from the way he goes about love. If the idea of being a typical Jewish couple makes him so afraid, it does so because for him it stands for that sacrilegious moment when the young Jewish boy, using his spouse as a substitute, is meekly married off to his mother.

But whether he resists, runs away or throws an angry fit by stamping his feet, Portnoy is never a happy rebel. It'll never work: there's too much love in its rawest form in his family, too much cumulative Jewish suffering for him to take refuge in the abrupt cutting of connections that ideology requires. Should he respond by politicizing the nuclear family? Should he make mommy/daddy into a symbol of the Old World, with its congenital pettiness and musty old values? Nothing works: his efforts at conceptualization are in vain, mommy and daddy resist the general concepts with which he tries to endow them. Work-family-country: the reactionary trilogy doesn't explain the functioning of his family. For his parents don't rely on the language of *authority*: they resort to the far more frightening languages of *affection* and of *Jewish history*. Standing up to a tyrant is infinitely preferable to facing these creditors claiming their tribute in love, or a spokesperson of a victimized people demanding a minimum of solidarity. Wrongdoer and the rebel are luminous roles, powerful heroes that Portnoy looks on with envy. He's the guilty one, always receiving more love than he returns. And no matter what he does, Portnoy is deprived of the healthy pleasures of transgression. His drama, in effect, is to have grown up in the bosom of a family whose ancestral tradition never let itself be reduced to force of law. Faced with parents who were sometimes unhappy but never repressive, he can lay no claim to the grand crime of disobedience; his less spectacular realm of possibilities consists of ingratitude, as if he were condemned to perpetual *treason*. Should he want to refute certain axioms of his education, love betrayed takes him to task. Should he seek to free himself from this very sort of love, a wounded Judaism cries out in humiliation and distress. The family and Judaism join together in an inextricable emotional knot.

It all began a century and a half ago with the assimilation of Western Jews. Hoping to be admitted into non-Jewish society, they didn't beat around the bush. We've seen the kind of enthusiasm they showed in conforming to the terms imposed by emancipation. Won over by the ideas of the Enlightenment, they proceeded on their own to dissolve a culture that no longer reflected them. Besides, they'd been asked to modernize, not to convert: why should they feel any remorse? These new-style Jews were comfortable with who they were. To them, the moral superiority of the France of the Rights of Man consisted of a welcome that required no such renunciation. And these same people who, at the end of the nineteenth century, were ignorant of almost every aspect of Judaism, had nothing but contempt for their fellow Jews who baptized their children. But without a Jewish nation (a burnt offering placed on the altar of assimilation), the family was entrusted with the task of perpetuating a sense of Jewishness. The famous "family-centrism" of the Jews was something like a counterweight to assimilation. By falling back on the family circle, by conferring on it a sort of affective preeminence, many Israelites resisted a cultural disintegration that they had otherwise initiated on their own.

And then (for we must always come back to it) there was the Holocaust. It was an event that had the double effect of accelerating the process of assimilation and depriving it of its *raison d'être*. Why identify with liberal Europe if it's only to end your life as a free man in a sealed-off train? And why as well, after Auschwitz, should you continue using a language and living a culture and way of life that makes you stand out, that turns you into a visible and therefore willing victim, into anger's meat? It was those miraculously spared by the Holocaust, those Jews of Eastern Europe, who took up the work of assimilation anew. It was these Polish, Hungarian, Rumanian or Russian immigrants, whose non-Catholic manners had been of such concern to their coreligionists, who became paragons of discretion at the end of war. Contrary to a line from a singer popular in the fifties, the crematoria were not incubators. There weren't enough foreign Jews in France for their presence to be perceived as an outrage, even counting the new arrivals: those who'd fled their country during Hitler's invasion and who rejected with disgust any idea of going back. Fewer in number, these immigrants were above all deprived of any cultural desires; the final solution had let them live, but shattered any will to transmit their heritage. The catastrophe was something like a break in the narrative of history: there was what happened before the Holocaust, and the aftermath. Its survivors didn't have the heart to bring the story to a tidy end.

But mere survival wasn't enough. You'd have to have come through the Nazi period untouched. Like a personal scar, like a painful memory, like a preface not to be inflicted on younger generations, the vanquished kept the treasure of Yiddishkeit for themselves. Everyone will tell you: they were exemplary. They participated in the baby boom and produced beautiful, healthy babies, outstanding and without any accent. Those who had faced the inferno had only one real wish: that nothing happen to their children. Their offspring must not look anything like the victims of extermination. Superstition? A lucid judgment? They were determined *not* to produce French-born Polish Jews, and imagined a secure and happy life for their children, not the fate of being abandoned or going to war. These anxious, uneasy, overprotective parents wanted above all to avoid getting in the way of school. Yiddish language, religious tradition – all that could come between their progeny and mandatory courses was mercilessly cast aside. Why? To avoid clouding their children's schoolwork with superfluous messages, to avoid overburdening their little intellects with a culture that had no *practical* use; in short, to avoid handicapping their children in the competition for diplomas. The survivors didn't feel up to contesting the school's intellectual monopoly, especially if their offspring were the stakes in the unequal struggle that would result. David gave in to Goliath, without even the slightest gesture of defiance or resistance. He did more: he became the giant's aide, an active and zealous agent of centralism, a fervent propagandist for the university's omnipotence. And we Jewish children were called on to undertake wonderful studies. Our charge, given us by our parents, was to be good students. They'd been careful not to overload our minds with knowledge that would sidetrack us; they'd left our capacities completely fresh so we'd learn without any wasted time and make unhindered progress. To better secure our chances of academic success and professional achievement, Judaism was willingly erased and sworn to silence.

Muteness and clamor; cries that were gagged. While Judaism's varied teachings were being silenced, what was insistently, *effusively* impressed upon us was the pride of being Jewish. These parents were assimilated in a way decidedly different from others: they said yes to the school's cultural monopoly, but no to the Israelite character. There was no worse indignity in their scheme of values than shame at being a Jew. Survival was already a betrayal of the dead; renouncing your origins would have been like killing them again. The children of survivors grew up in the shadow of funereal presences and accounts of atrocities. They were raised according to two equally rigorous and absolutely contradictory principles: one was conformity and personal ambition, and the other, intransigence and the cult of the dead. The family wanted them completely Jewish, but took care that none of their qualities might hinder their entrance into academic culture. The *Wunderkind* was the ideal type: the unusually gifted child who met the contradictory demands of loyalty to his kind and of brilliant success; the Child Prodigy who respected the law of endogamy even while, carrying all its baggage, he crossed over to the "other side." For here it's the family that demands the act of rupture and emancipation that will thrust their heir to the front of the crowd. The native milieu calls for its own abolition, as if – in a perverse version of the Oedipus complex – symbolic murder were filial piety in its purest form. These parents had but a single dream: to have children who didn't resemble them, to create *mutants* – proprietary owners of the French tongue, collectors of diplomas and intimates of knowledge. All the while, these beings from another world and another culture were to remain Jews *on the inside,* obsessed with their history and constantly aware of their identity.

It was a strange way to be Jewish: a Judaism without content, and a Judaism that was purely sentimental, a Judaism emptied of all substance by the very people who required it of you. A Jewish mutant is a weird kind of creature: the only proofs of belonging he can offer are his feeling for Judaism and his marriage. But whatever the case, the family is assured of its ultimate triumph. In their first period of assimilation, the family had been the Jewish people's last bastion against disappearance. The hearth substituted for an absent or at least scattered community, transmitting a kind of minimal Judaism. Today the hearth has come to be that very Judaism itself. For many of us, being Jewish is first and foremost the impossible relation sustained since childhood with our parents' contradictory demands: we're always *lagging,* never Jewish enough according to a standard of intensity held by them alone, never victorious enough to satisfy the dreams of happiness and grand ambition they dreamt on our behalf.

Whether through irritation or fatigue, I finally gave in and offered my Jewishness to psychoanalysis. If wishing doesn't make it so, why keep looking for Judaism at heights where it can no longer be found? Gone are the magnificent transports and professions of pathetic faith. In such reductionist moments I surrendered to the corrosive pleasures of vulgar analyses. I took transcendence in my hands and tore it apart. Jewishness, Judaism, Judaicity: in a rage I did away with fine distinctions, treated my Jewish identity as a common flower, something no better than a psychic quirk or neurosis. "What's Judaism? A passionate brawl, an endless guerrilla war, draining and unproductive, a (melo)dramatic interpretation constructed by parents and a little child who can no more join them than he can leave them behind. They want him for themselves, their eternal baby: Judaism is the name they give this desire for the sole purpose of making it presentable to the world! They lay their claim to me, and I stupidly discuss it with them, plead and equivocate, fall into their trap. They impose their demands, using the suffering of a people as their pretext, and I naively swallow their blatant blackmail. Oh, I know they're not Machiavellian, and if they make me *prove* my Jewishness once in a while, if they're so anxious about my allegiance, it's only out of panic and fear that the success of their own educational method has provoked. They created him – the mutant of their dreams – so they'd like him to pay back in exuberance and passionate proclamations what he's lost in cultural affinity. He must be a demonstrative Jew, he who no longer has anything Jewish about him, the perfect little Frenchman that he is. Such a *fear* I can understand. But that's the problem in a nutshell: isn't it wrong for me to understand? Isn't that the biggest trap of all? Isn't that what makes me an adult who's still swaddled in diapers, an infantile adult who'll never grow up? That's the 'judaic' tie that binds me, the tie that holds me. Fascinated with my Jewish identity, I succumb to *their* neurosis, playing a game whose rules they've invented, until I'm entangled in a desire that is not my own! Sartre clearly missed the mark on this one. I don't owe my Jewishness to the malevolent gaze of the Other but to the family's goodwill, the new ghetto. As for my supposed authenticity, it's nothing but a bunch of torments, precautions, prohibitions and faults I'm unable to leave behind."

This scowling monologue, however, doesn't get at the truth of my Judaism. I had scarcely invoked psychoanalysis before being seized by a desire to snatch back the gift about to be laid at its feet. *Portnoy cannot be reduced to the sum of his complaints.* Like characters in a vaudeville routine with me at its center, my parents also belong to another story in which I don't exist. As connected and bound to one another as we are, part of their being escapes me, and can't be contained in our little triangle. Though the family is everything to them, and in spite of their self-denial, they're more than members of a family. In their solidarity with a vanished people and as survivors of an invisible tragedy, they're not confined to our space but transcend, without really meaning to, "family life" and its obligatory impasses. As model parents they devote themselves to their child, it's true, but their excessive affection won't do any good. It doesn't matter that I'm marked by their imprint in everything I do, that they inhabit me, push me with their demands, encumber me with their image. For I'm still power-less to claim their uniqueness as my own. Their kind of Jew-ishness is forbidden me, and I, their next of kin, flesh of their flesh, contemplate it from afar.

Such crushing presences are also evasive presences, part of an impenetrable world. My fears and problems are no doubt born of our delirious intimacy, but psychology cannot begin to say what their estrangement means. For there are things be-yond memory that link me to this inviolable past, that connect me to a universe that will soon come to an end and disappear forever. There are the thousand things we don't have in com-mon that I'll never have a chance to acquire. There's the au-thenticity they preserved as an endowment all their own: a Ju-daism that *flows from the source,* an inimitable style, a certain way of living a culture, and that no account can change from the particular to the universal: the yellow star and the experi-ence of Nazism *as lived.* (Cioran: "Detailing, classifying and explaining the trials of someone who has suffered is always done in vain: what he is, his actual suffering, is beyond you. The more you approach him, the more he seems inaccessible to you.") There's the way they give me the fascinating feeling that I come from somewhere, though they were born in exile and hounded from it as well. There's something beyond all the words I've traversed (injunctions, reproaches, outpourings, sulkings), the sound of their *language,* the unique melody that is their inalienable possession and which they'll take with them as they go. There's the fact that they are the last wit-nesses of a Jewry that's deceased (Central European Jewry).

I am not Jewish, in short, because the Eternal One, the

Zionist ideal, the spirit of revolt or an Oedipal symptom are present within me. What makes me a Jew is the acute consciousness of a lack, of a continuous absence: my exile from a civilization which, for "my own good," my parents didn't wish me to keep in trust.

PART THREE
The Dispersed and Their Kingdom

7
The Dream of the Diaspora

They have a vagabond soul, the Western Jews. Their thoughts are in another place. The youngest, the generation that was preserved, virtuously assume their condition, trying to find ways to convince themselves that the amorphous and haphazard world in which they live is a totalitarian society, and that they are its potential pariahs. But catastrophe's survivors themselves succumb to the compelling power of the imaginary. While their children dress down in flashy outlaw outfits, they prefer to claim the stature of the sabra as their own. They've entrusted Israel with the task of representing Jewish existence. Since 1948, they've remained uneasy or entranced spectators watching their own legend unfold, seeing themselves as proxy pioneers, soldiers and farmers of the desert, as vicarious citizens of the Jewish state, identifying with the courage of the inhabitants of Israel in its glorious yet everyday form. There, in a minuscule and threatened land, Jews are at once the embodiment of their millenial destiny and avengers of their oppression. For the Diaspora, this faraway nation is like an inner kingdom, providing its subjects of anxiety, pride and conversation. A Diaspora of dreams.

THE SONS OF THE IMPOSSIBLE

Zionism in the past was not a projection but one *response* among many to the Jewish Question, a solution that presented itself as both an ideal and a response to the pressing problem of security. "Listen, Doctor, don't even talk to me about Judaism, I wouldn't wish it on my worst enemy. Slurs and Shame: that's all that comes of it. It's not a religion, it's a misfortune" (Heine). Zionism arose at the end of the nineteenth century to end this misfortune once and for all. Other therapies offered at the time had the same intent. A minority position, the Palestinian option drew opposition on several fronts: from liberal thinkers who prophesied the rising tide of civilization; from the religious orthodox, who regarded the wish to settle in the Holy Land as a sacrilege, unless a sign from the Almighty were given; from the revolutionary hope in the proletariat as the sole embodiment of the universal, which at the same time conferred on it the noble task of eradicating anti-Semitism; and finally from that Jewish version of socialism, the Bund, that was struggling for both the emancipation of the workers and for the Jewish right to national and cultural autonomy.[1] At times, these various global solutions even found common ground. There were, for example, Israelites who, while objecting to Zionism as an option for themselves, pleaded the Zionist cause for their unfortunate coreligionists in Eastern Europe. As for the extremely influential Left-Zionists, they dreamed of a socialist nation state and would join in the work of building the Land of Israel only if it were to be based on collectivist and egalitarian grounds.

Then came the final solution, more speedy than the rest, putting an end to compromise as well as confrontation. Jews who had placed their faith in European civilization or in the liberating power of the workers' cause had nothing to show for their trouble. Neither the universal value of reason nor the universal proletariat had been able to foresee, much less prevent Hitler. It was in the modern, educated West, with its philosophers and technology, that the blond brutes were unleashed: it was there they seized power and committed a crime whose horror is without parallel or precedent in human history. *Seen from Auschwitz,* it was not hope that had been lost: the very words *Progress, Humanism,* or *Revolution* seemed absurd, as if marked by an unredeemable futility. The same Jews who had mocked the Zionist project were now in agreement about its prescience and prophetic power. The Holocaust had turned their empirical theories into so many visionary dreams. They'd dismissed the mirage and were angered at their own incredulity, as if it were a criminal optimism or aberration. According to Isaac Deutscher, an early Bolshevik and later a Trotskyist:

> If instead of arguing against Zionism in the 1920s and 1930s I had urged European Jews to go to Palestine, I might have helped to save some of the lives that were later extinguished in Hitler's gas chambers.[2]

Former opponents of the doctrine of the ingathering of exiles now celebrated it in retrospect for its prophetic power. In 1948, few survivors would even dream of contesting Israel's right to exist. Zionism achieved universal acceptance, but it was a somber victory, and produced a tragic split. The Jewish state found its *raison d'être* in the annihilation of those for whom it had been envisioned: the persecuted communities of Eastern Europe. The Promised Land, in other words, would never have come to be if those Jews who had sworn to pursue it had not perished in the Holocaust. At the crucial moment, support had been vital, though it became clear only after the fact, when the emergency that made it necessary had passed. For Israel to be born, those who needed it most had to die.

Hence the apparent inconsistency of Western Jews: they're all Zionists, but they all stay settled right where they are. The occasional charge of double allegiance levied against them is useless, for it won't force them to choose. They see no contradiction between life in the Diaspora and love for Israel. The fact that the Jews are the majority somewhere is what allows them, in France and elsewhere, to live as a minority. For Hitler transformed the conception of anti-Semitism that Jews had previously held. Before the Holocaust, hatred was seen as a result of the wish for segregation, of a desire to isolate their little-understood nation, to stigmatize it and to set it apart.[3]

Faced with this discriminatory mindset, several responses were possible, ranging from religious nonviolence to self-defense, and including outright apostasy or total devotion to the revolutionary cause. After the Holocaust, however, measured distinctions are no longer possible. Any reticence soon evokes the camps: the most coded expressions of anti-Semitism are immediately seen by their victims as a *will to extermination*. Reasoning with the Jews or preaching to them is useless. A bunch of paranoids? Complacent? Prone to morbidity, or vanity? Perhaps: but the medico-moral approach won't do a thing. Confronted by intelligent yet amnesiac people adept at figuring out dosages, weighing, classifying and evaluating messages of hate, at categorizing them properly in an order that reflects their animating intensity, Jews have chosen stupidity and memory. They've become elephants. Inept at making distinctions, they deliberately lack subtlety and nuance. They lump finely wrought phrases together with mudslinging insults: "your people," uttered without any conscious malice, and the cruel or vulgar "Dirty Jew!" are treated as if one and the same. From harmless stereotype to assault to synagogue desecration, Jews flatten out every offense until it fits a single model: Auschwitz. Furiously, they even out all differences, in an obsessive and passionate kind of leveling. Whoever doesn't like them wants to kill them. Too bad for historical differences. No form of anti-Semitism can be entirely innocent of the Holocaust. Only a single recourse seems possible to this desire for extermination, apparent in each of our adversaries without exception: a Jewish homeland. The reason some choose not to emigrate to this salvific state is because the slaughter has already occurred, and the memory of its horror that surrounds them offers a protection stronger than even the force of arms. Without Israel, the slightest outbreak of anti-Semitism would immediately throw the Jews into an impotent panic that the past was about to repeat itself. Recent history has etched a double certainty into the Jewish consciousness: that the catastrophe could not happen again, and that Israel was needed to escape perpetual anxiety over its improbable return.

Militant Zionists seem discouraged by their own triumph. Everyone agrees with them and no one moves to Israel. What movement there is now takes place in the wrong direction – New York is not only the largest Jewish city, but also the second-largest Israeli city in the world. Zionism has conquered its opponents, and inertia has conquered Zionism. And some of its stalwarts don't mince words in criticizing what they see as defeatist behavior. The kindest terms deployed in their indictment are *deserter, old-fashioned,* and *coward.* The Diaspora's reasons for staying put, according to these died-in-the-wool types, can't be spoken in polite company. Like those progressives whose hearts are with the Left while their bank accounts are in Switzerland, Jews who hesitate seem to be congenitally incapable of squaring their everyday lives with their inflammatory pronouncements. It's an old but contradictory story: how can one claim that Jews will only be truly secure within Israel's borders, while at the same time criticizing them for preferring the easy life that keeps them from becoming its citizens? But perhaps the unfairness of this charge is largely the result of a careless use of words. The same word – *Zionism* – designates and confuses two divergent passions: the love of Israel and the wish to go there and live. Militants for *aliyah* (emigration) play on this semantic ambiguity to take the position of judge, placing their interlocutors in the position of traitor: they complain that obstinate members of the Diaspora haven't yet raised their actions to the level of their ideas. The Diaspora is accused of saying one thing while doing another, of supporting Israel to appease their conscience, thereby wiping out their deficiency and distance in a single stroke. The net result is to hold Jewish reality to a standard that no longer applies to its situation.

And in the massive support they give Zionism, Western Jews have demonstrated a loyalty deceiving in its scope (sometimes mystifying even themselves about their intentions). Heretics without recognizing themselves as such, they've surreptitiously turned Zionist ideology away from its ultimate goals. Zion is no longer the promised one, the fiancée and the future bride, but mother and child wrapped into one – the far-off mother whose simple existence is reassuring, who protects as well as produces a beneficial effect. Israel is her last born, the Benjamin of Jewish communities, the child prodigy whom you watch grow up, whose exploits you follow as your heart bursts with joy. "Next year in Jerusalem": a meaningless invocation now that Jerusalem is Jewish. Hope has been replaced by affection, as an invisible metamorphosis has turned Israel into this oddly filial and maternal figure, an absent presence who protects from a distance and fills her children and parents with pride – the Jews of the Diaspora.

What have they got to be so proud of? They're proud that Israel has challenged majority discourse and restored their good name. It was not so long ago that *Jew* had effectively become a special kind of reference, an automatically degrading image that its own models were powerless to change. Today we've reached the point where the stereotype has been cast aside by those it was meant to portray. Instead of protesting or hanging their heads, Jews relinquish the traitor or Shylock image to the hands of their detractors. Thanks to Israel, Jewish consciousness is gradually emancipating itself from the yoke of public opinion. The time of being-for-others is done. Now one can be a descendant of the prophets without having to be haunted by that spectral character: the image of the Jew created, described, promoted and given cultural authority by secular prejudice. Such confident disregard had not been seen since ghettos were left behind.

There have been other times, no doubt, in the days of rabbinic government and closed communities, when Jews could afford to ignore Others and face the animosity that surrounded them with a silent but unflinching scorn. Though they were subjected to hatred and vulnerable to attack, there was comfort to be found in the idea of their elect status, setting them apart from the culture and beliefs of their oppressors. The religious Jew could react with humility to the world's violence, for he was conscious of belonging to the people of the Covenant. His tolerance of oppression was but one face of a coin whose flip side was invincible obstinacy. The nation of Moses conceded everything to the dominant culture except the most important thing of all: the symbolic power that might have forced the Jews to accept its values, and which might have made them ashamed of being what they were. Judaism, then, inextricably mixed misfortune and consolation into one.

So what was emancipation if not precisely such a *change of alliance,* a sort of grand marriage of the Jews with their time? By leaving the ghettos and assimilating, the people of the Torah decided to fuse its law with that of the modern world. The walls fell that had been battlements as well as a prison; their divine mission no longer offered protection against everyday malignity, and this slander that language conveyed. *Jew* was still an insult, but no longer a refuge. With God increasingly distant, society took possession of Jewish identity and managed it with all of its power. The transition limited the Jews to two implacable alternatives: either reclaim their tradi-

tion by making something positive out of the defamatory label stuck to their backs, or beat their accusers at their own
game, by recognizing the standing of their tribunal and trying
to prove their case in order to have the charge dismissed. The
conflict between the Israelite and the Jew was born, as we have
seen, from such total dependence on the gaze and approval of
others. There were masters and there were slaves, and the
slaves were free only to choose between revolt or willing sub-
mission.

Is anti-Semitism in its death throes? Or is it on the contrary
experiencing a rebirth? That's the million-dollar question, and
the unanswerable question. While the Judeophobic gossips and
the force of their convictions remain in place, they've at least
been deprived of their monopoly. The good old days are gone
for good, and the anti-Semite is a monarch dethroned, imagining the Jew in terms he has long since ceased to consider as
significant. Why? Because there's a Jewish state, a Jewish army,
postage, money and a land that finally bears the Jewish stamp:
in short, because Israel creates a set of *collective images* that
prejudice is powerless to effect. Instead of entering into a con-
testatory dialogue with a portrait of himself drawn by his enemies, the Diaspora Jew now has the power to transcend it and
identify directly with the Israeli image.

He does this with an eagerness sometimes judged to be too
passionate, a newly minted and harmful indulgence. For the
soft-touch father of the Diaspora, the world revolves around
Israel, his little baby. He loves it for all sorts of reasons, both
good and ill, admirable and trivial. His overflowing affection
admits of no division, not even the *minimally Manichaean split*
between the right and the left. It's an excitable tolerance quick
to celebrate the least compatible qualities, indiscriminately
glorifying the raid on Entebbe and the virtues of the pioneers,
the adventure of the kibbutzim and the efficiency of the Israeli
Defense Forces, the gains made toward achieving a utopian

society and the economic conservatism of the various governments.

Such continual chauvinism has long been a source of irritation to me. I would have hoped my parents and their generation could have been more moderate, and above all more
selective in their enthusiasms. As a child born in peacetime, I
experienced their happiness without understanding its grounds.
What did I want? For them to be leftists, to support Israeli socialism, and to repudiate militarism with a will that was
equally strong? For me, everything was simple: there was
nothing except the right and the left, no aspect of reality that
escaped its dualistic terms. My experience of anti-Semitism,
moreover, had been too fleeting and too sporadic to disturb
this vision of the world. Their euphoria, which I treated as a
matter of political choice, was in fact a response to other mo-
tivations and other criteria. The loyalty that seemed so undis-
criminating to me was, in fact, quite natural once one looked
beyond the categories of ideology: every aspect of Israel was a
bit of dignity returned to the Jews as a whole. The farmer of
the Negev erased the image of the lender, the flowering desert
erased the image of the parasite, and the Israeli soldier served
as proof that *Jew* and *coward,* or *Jew* and *victim,* are not syn-
onymous terms. As for the islands of communal socialism,
they were peopled with Jews whose proper and typical goal
was to renounce money, not to enrich themselves. Those who
sympathized with the new state were so thoughtlessly supportive only because they had been crushed by attacks that were
the opposite of the picture that Israel represents. It didn't matter a bit whether some aspect of Israeli life were characteristic
of the left or the right: they bought it every time. Anti-Semitism had always transcended this political opposition that we,
the youngest of the young, saw as all-encompassing.

Israel: a redemptive country that rescues Jews from the influence of their detractors. This is why certain Zionists feel a

rapturous astonishment at having a state *like any other*. Normalcy itself becomes a kind of deliverance, liberating Jews from the need to prove themselves. Look at them now, freed of the excessive and relentless loyalism that one hundred and fifty years of assimilation had made instinctive. Look at them now, relieved of the burden of a Jewish character that consisted, as they put it, of being like everybody else, only a little more so: how true it is that the copy is always better than the original it imitates, for fear of being seen as false or unfaithful. By lending them an image at once ordinary and heroic, and by allowing Jews to take the best of both worlds – a *heroic* one and a *mediocre* one – Israel put Jews at ease. Anti-Semitic passion no longer has anything to latch onto, and while it can try to regain its lost influence by fighting the racketeers and conspirators it discovers under every bed, the thrill is gone. Jews feel exonerated of any imaginary anomaly that can be laid at their feet. They no longer need to become *too* normal to give certain proof to themselves and others that they clearly belong to the human race. What Israel gave them is a sort of moral ease, the taste of an unknown calm. These are souls no longer haunted by terror as before, nor governed by that crushing imperative: Don't stand out.

Let's think back on 1967, the spectacular inaugural date when Jews broke with the *politics of the invisible*. With De-Gaulle denouncing Israel's actions, the Jewish population rose in unanimous revolt against the French government. What a transgression! What an unbelievable novelty! Never since the founding of the Republic had the Jews of France dared to take a position in such peremptory fashion, especially where their own coreligionists were concerned. Rallying in solidarity had once been a test, a moment of truth, a kind of visibility that could turn into a trap: the risk, in a word, of reviving the old image of the Jewish nation, with its cabals and its secret networks. When Bernard Lazare pleaded for his community's support to obtain the retrial of the Dreyfus case, the majority turned nervously or indignantly away from this irresponsible man, this energumen whose agitating ways threatened an already precarious civil tranquillity. Such was the great irony of the Dreyfus affair: on one side stood the co-alition of the army, the civic groups and the clergy, decrying the conspiracy, denouncing the Dreyfus "syndicate's" hold on France, and blaming each of its defeats on the all-powerful Jewish faction. On the other side stood the Jews themselves, as Léon Blum relates, thinking only of hunkering down, hid-ing out and preparing itself, adds Péguy, to sacrifice one of their own to quell the storm.[4] Fear overshadowed any feeling of kinship, fear and the additional sense that this was an op-portunity not to be missed: wouldn't the Jews be cleared of all suspicion if they ostensibly kept their distance from a racial brother? Two birds could be killed with one stone: "by giving up the goat," they bargained for peace, and were cleansed of the crime of helping their own.

> For every three dozen people in France you might have found to defend one of their martyred brothers, you would have found thousands willing to stand guard around Devil's Island with the most devoted champions of the na-tion.[5]

The rise of Nazism made no perceptible difference in this state of affairs. Licking the hand that struck them, Dreyfus's contemporaries donated forty thousand francs to Catholic charities amidst an outburst of hatred against the people who killed Christ; thirty years later their sons were greeting Colo-nel de La Roque, leader of the Croix de Feu, within the con-fines of the synagogue on Rue de la Victoire, so concerned with keeping a low profile that they shrank back in horror at the prospect of a campaign against Nazism. The word of the day was simple: have confidence in the State, let secret diplomacy do its work, pray and be quiet. The politics of fear and of appeasement led immigrants to scorn Jewish institutions, as this sarcastic commentary attests:

> It is this fearful concern to be more royalist than the king, more Catholic than the Pope that makes us believe that to be good Frenchmen, one must always be in agreement with the current Minister of Foreign Affairs.[6]

The Arab-Israeli conflict of 1967 was thus the decisive moment when things could have gone either way. The Jews of France chose unanimously to come out of the shadows and to insist, at their risk and peril, on the difference between France and the French government. They did for the sake of Israel what they had not done for Dreyfus or for the Jews of Yiddishkeit, or, by the way, for themselves. "The Israelis are not a continuation of the Israelites, they are their metamorphosis" (André Malraux).

And so it was that the Jews needed Israel to cure them of anxiety and shame, which in turn enabled them to admit without hesitation their attachment to Israel. The Diaspora was indebted to the Jewish state for this minimal assurance, the degree zero of bravery: the courage to speak *out loud*. (Sartre, in his *Reflections on the Jewish Question,* reports a small but awful fact. In an article written at the time of the Liberation, he had enumerated the victims of the war, finding room among the prisoners and political detainees to mention Jewish suffering. As a result, he received many letters expressing gratitude, so astonished were the Jews, even those returning from the camps, that someone was willing to break the code of silence and had begun a dialogue with them.) The Six Day War put an end to two centuries of resignation, services held in secret and self-censorship. And let's recall that apathy posed a real danger. Jews mobilized with such speed to defend the very existence of Israel, not to support some disputed policy. At the

root of their sense of shock lay the fear of genocide. An un-
justified fear? Beware, for the wisdom of hindsight is cheap.
Nothing is written in stone; we must be ready for anything:
the outcome of an event is not legible in the event itself. No
one knew at the beginning of the war who was going to win,
and Arab propaganda spoke freely of annihilating Israel, two
facts that were enough to justify the anxiety shown.

Never had the attachment of Diaspora Judaism to Israel re-
vealed itself to be so deep. Nor had Zionist ideology ever been
faced with such a glaring contradiction. Where were the people of the Book in danger? In the very asylum created to place
them out of harm's way. Israel's fundamental affective state is
the risk of death; the affective state of the Diaspora – at least in
the West – is peace of mind. Nothing says, of course, that this
opposition is permanent, or that Israel cannot one day recover
its role as refuge. At the moment, in any case, the Jewish state
and Jews in exile have switched roles, but *discourse about them
has not changed in kind:* contemporary Zionism suffers from a
split between feeling and expression. Many among us go on as
if nothing were wrong, praising the Promised Land for a security that only life in the Diaspora can offer. Unshakable, they
keep presenting Israel as a *solution,* when, in reality, it is the
central site where Jewish existence continues to be a *problem*.

The connection of Zionist ideology to the sentimental Zionism of Jews of the Diaspora is thus based on a misunderstanding. For, today, love for Israel is all the more *intense* as its
prospects remain *uncertain*. The powerful word in the expression "the Jewish state" is the word *Jewish,* and not the word
state. 1948, 1967, 1973: three conflicts pit David/Israel
against all the Arab nations. 1975: the condemnation of Zionism by the majority of nations of the world. At each turning
point in its history, Israel seems to bring the Jewish condition
back to life. They're free citizens, aren't they, the sabras of Tel-
Aviv or of Galilee? Of course, but more importantly, they're

Jewish, *more Jewish than us*: singled out for universal op-probrium, they lead a chancy existence, the very life whose rigors Diaspora Jews (for the time being at least) no longer know. The epic of Israel is more than just a political tale. It cannot be told in terms of economic development, class strug-gle, social consensus or the relations carried on between states. Occasionally, it's true, Jews on the outside make use of such language, criticize the specifics of Israeli diplomacy, feel bad about the ethnic conflict that divides the country or dream up miraculous remedies for inflation. But it's just a temporary loan, a matter of inconsequentially abandoning yourself to the mundane concerns of everyday prose. The heart of the matter lies well above and beyond the political realm in which its concerns seem to play themselves out. Israel renders our categories for narrating its saga obsolete. This state like all others has the unique ability to chart a perpetually exceptional destiny. Its isolation and uncertain future are per-ceived as signs of an eternal curse. The Diaspora, seated front row, watches the continuation as well as the transformation of its own history. The Jewish state is that mythic character that joins the roles of victim and hero into one. In spite of its secu-lar manifestations, Zion – orphan and avenger – proves to all the world's Jews that their adventure is unfinished and that their uniqueness has not yet toed the line.

Israel, since its founding, has known but a single state: *the state of emergency*. And so the Jews of the Diaspora, for the most part, decline all offers to relax. The critical tribunal is in recess. So long as peace for Israel remains in doubt, the Israeli venture can tolerate neither restrictions nor conditions. It is beyond all debate, removed from any rational examination or control, and Jews think of their relationship to the Jewish state in military terms. As part of the populace who live in the rear, they aren't about to carry indecency to the point of foist-ing advice or heaping criticism on those who live *at the front*.

On the contrary, they will try to atone for that distance by spanning their geographic distance from the theater of operations with an unconditional support that passes every test. Yes, always yes, it's the least we can do while we watch events unfold on television.

This unconditional support for every Israeli policy is the symptom of a malaise. The Diaspora, prey to a vague sense of guilt, compensates with vehement loyalty. Absence makes the heart grow fonder, and Jews in exile exorcize their historical situation by sticking to the official Zionist line, indeed, by taking it one step farther. There's also something more serious than their material comforts to be atoned for: the pleasure they take in watching Israel exist in the face of every peril and risk it can handle. As a genuine member of the contemporary world, it's a country placed in an extraordinary situation since its birth. Isolation and a precarious situation are largely responsible for making it more than simply some Boy Scoutish province of Jewish life. Yet as authentic as their uneasiness might be, Jews on the outside receive a whole series of important benefits from this vulnerability. They get a taste of how it feels to undergo mobilization, as they watch this lonely and rebellious nation-state write a new chapter in Jewish history instead of concluding it, which would certainly be desirable but hardly novelesque. Of the many anxious pleasures they enjoy, the crown jewel for Diaspora Jewry is the lucky stroke of having charged Israel, that country on the globe that *always makes the front page*, with the task of defining and representing them. For it's Israel that's always page-one news, and Israel that always makes the headlines. Such audiovisual permanence allows the Diaspora to survive its own cultural extenuation.

Just as important as the actual return to the land is the function it serves as world entertainment. The media effectively satisfy two contradictory desires in the Jewish populace: to enjoy a unique history (*histoire*), but without all its stories (*histoires*), with their mighty, enduring and painful memories of oppression. Without beliefs, community or a culture to call their own, Jews nonetheless salvage an identity from this triple catastrophe. They hold on to something imperishable: the news. Reading the newspaper takes up where religious observance left off, providing Diaspora Jewry with a daily feeling of attachment to the Israeli people as a whole. Now there are two types of practicing Jew: the devout who attend synagogue, and the much more numerous group who produce a running (and delectable) commentary on the situation in the Middle East as their form of observance. What do the oil embargo, the Camp David accords or the Islamic revival actually mean to assimilated Jews in Europe or America? Constant recognition, and a regular reminder of their condition. And what would happen if things took a turn for the better? If instead of being one of the world's hot spots, Canaan joined Switzerland and Belize in that privileged group of countries whom television ignores? Jews of the world would be united, no doubt, by a feeling of immense relief and genuine happiness. But it's just as certain that they'd feel as if something had been lost, for they would have been forced to abandon their last liturgical rite. For the problems that make the Jewish state an object of debate are received as a series of gratifying images, becoming material for an authentic religious practice. To be a hero by proxy, to ritualize the present, to need the insecurity of Israel to remain Jewish: each of these things explains why many in the Diaspora confusedly punish themselves through an unqualified solidarity with every decision that Jerusalem takes.

THE HUMILIATED AND THE GUILTY

Israel: the Jewish Zorro, cowboy with calloused hands. It's spectacular revenge on the image of the plutocrat or the shirker. Yet the children of the survivors had never suffered enough to feel the need for vengeance, hadn't experienced daily humiliation and knew of it only by hearsay. For them the external world was a blank. A few incorrigibles, to be sure, punctured the silence, but it wasn't enough to rouse a society that remained mute. Here or there an insult, sometimes an indistinct murmur, some off-color jokes, but all told, it was small game: the cursed aura they provoked was too intangible to provoke any desire for revenge. Jews who came after the horror had no score to settle with Western conscience or the majoritarian gaze. Why should Israel's sovereign machismo make any difference to those who'd never been accused of being cowards?

What fascinated them was the contrast between their gentle, womblike existence and the unrivaled history their identity implied. These were the children of Auschwitz and of the banana split, cherubic babes of a nation sentenced several years before their birth to absolute death. Their hope was to find some sense of connectedness, to heal the break, to carry the burden of the Just for the generation that had come just before. Three faces of Judaism presented themselves, but only one was compelling: the Israelite was hardly appealing, that French caricature with his ornate language and the refinement of a butler; and to the Israeli bursting with health and vigor, they preferred the Jew, unquestionable symbol of subjugated man.

These were young people, in other words, whose identity and way of life conflicted with one another. They weren't so much *humiliated* by violent prejudice as they were *guilty* about the Jewish tragedy. Their wish: to strengthen their sense of belonging, to be adequate to its demands, and since the wound of being Jewish had been spared them, to work on behalf of current victims of oppression to the point of living their misfortune. Born after the fact, exempted from Jewish destiny by the kindness of time, the last-minute martyrs made up for their tardiness by being finicky about their Jewish sensitivity. Colonized peoples fighting for their independence, Black Power, the Third World reconquering its dignity: these were, for them, the new Jews of history. Like everyone else, they spoke of imperialism, the pillaging of raw materials and the subjugation of the worker, but this Marxist discourse kept silent about the true nature of their support. What tied them to the plight of the Asians, the blacks, and the Bougnoules was the name forced upon them by their masters, not the material exploitation they suffered.[7] These were men excluded from humanity by the racist arrogance of the West, who paid for their skin color, that indelible yellow star.

A strange misunderstanding: to remain faithful to the experience of their parents, these children would submit to being treated as renegades. For Jews, the generational conflict that reached its peak in May '68 and in the hyperpolitical years that followed was an imaginary conflict before anything else. Who is the legitimate heir to the mantle of Jewish identity? Israel or the victims of the White Man's genocidal power? What is more Jewish: the construction of a Western enclave in the Middle East or the uprising of the downtrodden, the about-face of the damned of the earth? That was the question, and for a time it produced terrible disagreements.

It's worthwhile recalling, in fact, what the political climate of the sixties was like. The world is still clearly split into two camps. The USSR, it's true, has already lost its preeminence. After the revelations of the Twentieth Congress and the invasion of Hungary, it's just not the same. Even if the land of socialism still has its staunch supporters, it no longer has a monopoly on revolution, and no longer stands as the embodiment of the claims of suffering humanity. But this drawback doesn't cast anyone into confusion, for the duel goes on: another fresh-faced, messianic adversary stands up to the West. This new personification of hope is the Third World, which sees imperialism as its principal enemy and which rejects its white mask, that is to say the self-image that its former masters had tried to make it assume. It's a tumultuous and clarifying moment that admits of no equivocation: you have to choose sides. Israel's unconditional supporters castigate their young who are tempted by the revolution to turn against their origins; the bolshevik apprentices blame their parents for identifying with the actions of the Yankee as world policeman, and thus failing the test their own principles had set.

"We are all German Jews!" I've already described the rather stupid displeasure I'd felt on hearing this slogan announced. I adored the word *Jew,* wore it like a ring, and was enraged at seeing it become a piece of jewelry anyone could wear. The snob in me who loved his Judaism for its distinctive value protested against its sudden democratization. It was a rage that made me something like the aristocrat who watches his privileges being dismantled, spitefully branding the process decadence, or better yet (if he is on the Left), calling it the one-dimensionality and grievous sameness imposed on different ways of life. But for a number of Jewish adolescents, this malaise found its compensation in a feeling of jubilation. Self-righteously, they rejoiced in the chance to call the community's good conscience into question. Suddenly, they could discover and proclaim that they were more Jewish than their Zionist parents, whose constant refrain was nothing but Israel, Judaism and "the whole world's against us." As they marched with everyone else, young Jews slipped a coded message into the common rhetoric, one they knew only members of their family would understand. It went something like this: "We are all German Jews, lepers, stateless and banished, while you're no longer anything more than well-to-do burgomasters and ersatz Israelis, two-bit American flunkies and patriots of the most banal kind . . . Our revolt is Jewish, but the same can't be said of your Israeli chauvinism and of the remnants of your Israelite fear . . . Stop judging us in the name of an identity that you handle with care, but which we, on our own, have the courage to proclaim without shame, an identity we claim more boldly than you do yourselves. The true renegade is not who they think."

Che versus Moshe Dayan: some cited the various figures available for representing human oppression, and others the land of Israel. Everyone had his Jew. It was a battle of the stars – until the day arrived when the fedayin replaced the guerrilla fighter at the forefront of revolutionary combat. It was then that the war between the generations reached its peak. Thunderstruck, the Zionists saw their prodigal children take the side of the enemy in the very name of the Jewish idea! If only they were open about abandoning Judaism when they turned against their people! No, the perjurers claimed to be more orthodox than their fathers. They rallied, in the fight against what was described as a warlike, expansionist nation, to the defense of a wandering people, a people in Diaspora: the Palestinians, those universal exiles. Categories born of Jewish history were henceforth not to be applied to the victors, but to those whom they had despoiled.

Rosa Luxemburg didn't approve of people making too much of their Jewish blood. "It's impossible," she said, "to keep a special little corner in my heart for the ghetto." Assimilated Jews had this in common with internationalist Jews at the turn of the century: they played no favorites. They lived in the universal, and hoped to become advocates for all mankind. Given the importance of such a mission, why should they be burdened with tribal notions and privileged ties to the Jewish community, that village of their birth? The leftists of the sixties were no Rosa Luxemburgs. As genocide's inheritors, they couldn't be satisfied with treating the suffering of the ghetto as a minor trial or just another problem. Instead it became a kind of absolute standard against which all other human horrors were to be measured. Invoking the experience of the ghetto became a means of expressing their anger against the Jewish state and excommunicating Israel. The symbol of the Jews, according to them, had changed hands. The Palestinians cooped up in refugee camps were now the rightful owners of the yellow star.

Many intermediate positions were staked out between the extremes of intransigent Zionism and unconditional support for the Palestinian cause. Few Jewish revolutionaries, in fact, were untroubled by attempts to distinguish between the idea of Israel and the nation that bore its name. Yet there were limits to the work of abstraction: the Jewish idea was not easily separated from living Jewish communities, even if those communities didn't seem to be living up to their calling. As a result, the extreme Left produced its own marranos, Israelophobes on the outside who were secretly pro-Israeli.[8] The annals of the Communist League and *Liberation* are full of anecdotes that might seem odd or regrettable today, stories about these false converts who had long encouraged the invincible struggle of the Palestinian and who, during the Yom Kippur War, kept their ears glued to transistor radios, consumed with anxiety for Israel's survival. Defying their own proselytizing, and almost in spite of themselves, they resisted the idea they had so glibly defended: a democratic, secular and religiously pluralistic Palestinian state. They found consolation for this contradiction by telling themselves that they supported a far-off, utopian and improbable cause. Nothing would have disturbed this messianism more than the realization of its promise, and the victory over Israel by the revolutionary Messiah.

As for me, I made use of an expedient other than hypocrisy. By chance I came across a rhetoric that reconciled, without too much damage, what at the time was called the desire for revolution with what I didn't yet dare call my need for faith.

This elite, high-powered Marxism was imported from Italy. Its distinguishing feature, more than its obscure jargon, was a horror of revolutionary exoticism. To this ultra-elite ultraleftism, the tropical reveries that dominated all brands of oppositional politics were the height of stupidity. For history had but one subject: the worker of the multinational proletariat, confronted with the naked truth of abstract labor, freed of all notions of social mobility and from any archaic attachment to job or to trade. Such a worker didn't attack the employers and carry the banner of the socialist state, but rejected the very foundation of capitalist society, labor itself. He wanted everything right away – no need for mediation, for he was communism in action, a dagger aimed at the very heart of the great capitals of Industrial Society. In other words, salvation would not come from the margins (i.e., the Third World), but from the center (i.e., Europe or America), the countries where we lived. What a windfall for the militant Jew! I was finally safe from dominant Third-Worldism and its endless demands that I cut myself off from what was dearest to my heart. I helped myself by out-lefting such inquisitorial discourse, criticizing it as weak and a distraction from the real issues. I praised the communism of the working class (we called it the Class) as superior to the regressive socialism of the worker's movement, privileging the Marx of the *Grundrisse* over Louis Althusser's, valuing its refusal to work over the Stakhanovism of all existing revolutions. As for the rest, I was off duty: my attachment to Israel was my own concern. Sentimental Zionism was just like taste in foods, or emotional outlook. Such choices belonged to the untouchable preserve of private preference and its shades. They weren't to be talked about. Anything that didn't directly concern worker autonomy was part of a category outside politics: a lesser pastime, like the pleasures of a soldier on leave.

All these tricks already seem like the legacy of a vanished

time. Five or six years have gone by, and we've almost forgotten the militant vocabulary, the litanies of the Left, the rites of the *manifs* (demonstrations), and the fact that dissenting youth were once part of the elite. History now has a different look, having abandoned the messianic aura of the revolutionary idea. So many popular uprisings have turned into dictatorships that we've ceased believing that the entire meaning of history concentrates itself in an existing historical situation, a universal class or a completely disinherited people. No revolutionary regime delivers on all the fabulous promises of its revolutionary movement, but until quite recently the phenomenon was of little concern. We simply remarked that a particular class (lacking in universality) had seized power, and looked elsewhere for the subject of history, farther away or lower down. It was a perpetual marketplace, and its most supportive and well-traveled salesmen ended up losing faith. Returning dead tired from an imaginary voyage that lead from Africa to China, with stops in Cuba and Southeast Asia, not to mention the great factories of capitalist overdevelopment, these globetrotters of the revolution no longer wished to rely on one part of humanity to decide the fate of the whole. The game of all or nothing was at an end.

Gradually, we came to terms with the notion that the historical universe is not an abstract world of exaggerated choices and absolute decisions, and accepted 1) that the desire for a reconciled society is in itself totalitarian; 2) that we live in the *relative,* and that we must take care to remain there; 3) that there are necessary battles but no telos, nor any harmony on the horizon; 4) that the idea of a universal class doesn't hold up: "We are always victims of an interior gulag when we cling to a dream of crystal" (Bukovskii). Yet verbal terror requires just such a dream. Without utopia, any kind of arrogance or inquisition becomes impossible. And now, for the first time, *utopia is missing*: we're no longer able to decide what must die as part of the old order and what represents the just life in the future to come. Such is the reason, no doubt, that tolerance has ceased being a ridiculous or forbidden word. Young Jews on the Left are no longer forced into the difficult situation of having to give carte blanche to the Palestinians, or of having to identify with their struggle in order to prove they're on the right side of history. And conversely, they can declare their attachment to Israel without necessarily supporting every decision its government takes.

Revolution (or the hegemony of politics) was two things: taking sides and imminence; the forcing of reality into a bipolar structure and the self-certainty that we lived in a decisive historical epoch when everything was about to change. We were creating a new world, and our name for this blessed maternity was modernity. Are we still in the modern period, or is the modern, on the contrary, an outdated category for describing a reality that's already in flux? Whatever the case may be, we live in a time of perplexity that no longer takes itself to be the center of history. The present no longer dominates our values, and Jewishness, following the trend, is no longer reducible to being committed to revolution or to Israel; it's now a matter of memory as well. Ever since the grand, intoxicating illusion of living at a turning point in universal history disappeared, our generation has become anxious about Jewish history and receptive to its past. For what did our politics really mean to us? A wild and excessive value placed on the here and now, a sense of urgency and of fulfillment. The feeling abandoned us, left us bereft and uncertain, transforming our relationship to Judaism. Instead of feeling its richness within us, we experienced only an insatiable lack, knew little of an almost nonexistent heritage, and were seized by a boundless, loving, and worried interest in even the slightest detail of a Jewish life that will never exist again – the glories and sorrows of the life of the Valorous of Cephalonia, the Salonica ghetto or the Jews of North Africa. We became curious about the rabble of Odessa, or the life of Bena Krik, King of the Jewish underworld, as recounted by Issac Babel. The autonomous and organized life of Polish communities, those genuine stateless societies. About the shaping force of Yiddish, which is not so much what linguists would call a language as it is a gestural code, a melody and a special sensibility. ("All this German, Hebrew, French, English, Slavonic, Dutch, Rumanian and even Latin is seized with curiosity and frivolity once it is contained within Yiddish, and it takes a good deal of strength to hold all these languages together in this state.")[9] This desire for knowledge took us by surprise; we had thought ourselves born to look straight ahead, the future was our element, our passion, our sustenance – and here we were all of a sudden completely preoccupied with renewing our broken ties and exhuming lost worlds.

THE CENTRALITY OF ISRAEL?

We're out of practice. Our training has been in politics, not in memory, and our first attempts at moving from one to the other have been marked by signs of awkwardness and incompetence. There's no question about our good intentions, but old reflexes are hard to shake: we abandon politics by giving the left/right divide a universal import, and by viewing history as a strictly modern concern. We annex the Jewish past and make it part of Israel's present, and we can think of culture only in terms of conflicting ideologies. There's no better example of this double colonization than the current fate that has befallen the illustrious distinction between Sephardic and Ashkenazi Jews.

The division between the "Spanish" and the "Germans," and more generally between Jews of the Mediterranean and those of Eastern Europe, was codified in the Middle Ages. It's been part of Jewish life ever since, with numerous stories carrying traces of the prejudice and sense of foreignness that these rival factions of the House of Israel have felt for one another. Read the beautiful *Nicolo Peccavi* by Armand Lunel, and you will see a tranquil Jewish community of the Comtat Venaissin, absolutely horrified, in 1769, at the arrival "of one of those bands of Teutonic Jews, all disreputable people, beggars and vagabonds, more frightening for our communities than an epidemic."[10] Take a look as well at Mangeclous, the hero of Albert Cohen, railing against "those Polish Jews with their jargon of woe, eaters of cold carp," those "men of the snow countries who do not know how to pronounce aright the words of our Holy Law!"[11]

It falls to Israel, in defiance of its own principles, to have transformed this divide into a social confrontation and ethnic problem. The founders of Zionism and members of the first immigrant wave, the Ashkenazim, dominate the country's political life. Meanwhile the Sephardim, at least those with North African origins, are both disdained and exploited by their coreligionists. What was previously a conflict between communities holding different beliefs is now a split between a political left and right, the proletariat and the bourgeoisie: Israel has politicized the difference between two civilizations, and we, in response, create a hallucinatory vision of Jewish history, forcing it into categories drawn from the Israeli example. A new left, in fact, has emerged in the heart of the Diaspora, not anti-Zionist but anti-Ashkenazi, rewriting collective Jewish memory as a dualistic story, consisting of the eternal conflict and contradiction between masters and rebels. It's a Marxism that's still kicking, refitting its tattered outfit with mystical and prophetic material, and casting the Sepharadim – those Easterners of the West, outcasts among a people of pariahs, and Jews to the second power – as Judaism's messiahs.

"Ashkenazi or simply a Nazi?" my close school friend asked

me one day with a faint smile. He was surmising, no doubt, that my variety of Judaism gave me no claim to moral superiority, and he wasn't shy about proving the point to me each time Israel got itself into a bind. There it was – around 1965, when we must have been seniors in high school – an opportunity that was too good to be true. *Le Monde* had just published a long exposé by Eric Rouleau on Israel's domestic problems, with a stunning result: the words *Ashkenazi* and *Sephardic,* previously known only to experts on Jewish life, had entered the political vocabulary of the West. And a grand entrance it was. It was then that we discovered racism to be a greater threat to the unity of the people of camp survivors than war, and learned that Israel had its own blacks, the Moroccan Jews. The question has been a familiar one to us ever since, and it's no longer possible to avoid an intolerable fact: Israel suffers from discrimination just like the rest of the world. But outrage over injustice can itself lead to a kind of blindness. Such is the case with the new Jewish left, both radical and reverent as it wages its merciless struggle against Ashkenazi hegemony, without a bad thing to say about the centrality of Israel to Jewish life. The Ashkenazim are identified with domination, and the Sepharadim with exclusion. A specific and localized exercise of power is treated as if it were an eternal and all-encompassing form of violence. The State has become everything; a people that survived two thousand years without temporal protection locates all its sustenance and meaning in the experiences of a state not yet thirty-five years old.[12]

Simply a Nazi? Let's bracket our fascination with Israel for a moment and try to understand the situation. When Monsieur de Maussane discovers that his daughter Aude intends to marry the Jew Solal, he finds consolation for the *mésalliance* by telling himself that at least the kidnapper isn't named Isaacsohn or Gouggenheim. It's 1930. This apparently inadvertent detail slipped into the first novel of Albert Cohen gives an accurate picture of the political climate in the decade that had just begun. After several years in remission, anti-Semitic feeling is once again on the loose in France. The postwar period is coming to an end and the *Ostjuden,* rolling into France in uncontrollable hordes, are the favorite targets of a growing fascist movement. These stateless immigrants, of course, provide an ideal explanation for the evils afflicting the nation: as peerless speculators, they become the providential culprits of the depression. Cosmopolitan by destiny and inclination, their contagious presence weakens the national ideal; quarrelsome out of what is finally excessive egotism, they incite war by pitting France against the kindly Germany of Chancellor Hitler. If you had to be Jewish in these troubled times, it was better to hail from the sunny South than from the Northern mists: better to be named Solal and not Weintraub or Zeigermacher.

Is the moral of this story that yesterday's downtrodden are the victors of today, and that the Cukiermans, those kings of Zion, now have the Solals shining their shoes? The situation is far more complex. Solal, a Jew from Corfu, would receive a king's welcome in Israel, suffering no more than Jews of Portuguese, Canadian, American, Dutch or French extraction whose ancestors fled Spain after the expulsion edict of 1492. The Israeli elite doesn't reject the Sephardim as a group, but — and here is the aggravating circumstance — it does reject Jews who have long resided in Islamic countries, and whose customs have been marked by their stay.[13] It's the Arab in them, in fact, that they detest, just as the Israelites of London or Paris of fifty years ago rejected the inner Jew that distinguished their coreligionists from Eastern Europe, landing in the middle of the West with their weird habits, polar faces, exotic cuisine and revolting dialect. The epoch of assimilation gradually replaced the traditional split between Ashkenazim and Sephardim with an opposition a thousand times more volatile, a split that brought self-policing Jews and openly Jewish Jews into conflict. On the one side, whether Spanish or German by origin, stood the denominational, self-repressed Judaism of liberal Europe. Standing opposite was the vulgarly obvious – vulgar because it was obvious – culture of Yiddishkeit. These Jews whom nobody wanted – the Repkowskis, Feigelbaums and Rosenblums who make up the endless roll of the massacred, that our disaffection with Israel imagines to be the Jews of the West, the privileged ones who abandoned their brethren as pariahs. It's too much.

✡

Israel gave our parents a pleasure whose taste they'd forgotten: the pleasure of being Jewish. No more excuses, dissimulation, or hidden fits of self-contempt. Israel let them live again, in public, in loving union with their image of Jewish destiny. For them, Zion wasn't a practical center; they'd chosen to remain in exile when the opportunity arose to bring it to an end. Nor was it the spiritual center that Ahad Ha'am dreamed of, but more precisely an imaginary center. The Diaspora followed the news from Israel, experiencing the dramatic trials and tribulations of the Jewish state in the first person: its exploits, its accomplishments, its grief and its obsidional complex as a nation under siege.

But we're not Jews who've been sinned against or humiliated: we're empty Jews. We don't suffer from hostile surroundings, but from our own inconstancy. We don't need a better image, just a little more memory. *Jew* designates the vacant space of a past that has become a tabula rasa. That's why we must free Israel of its charge. Not contest its legitimacy, of course, or renounce the defense of its existence, but refuse it the position of monopoly. Our Jewishness is so weak that the obsession with Israel imprisons us: it shapes our viewpoint and dictates our past. We are burdened by a forged memory that's nothing more than the Israeli present in disguise. No doubt the centrality of Israel has had beneficial and liberating effects. But if we aren't careful of its perverse results, our own history will gradually be lost. Between our individual problems and the retrospective imperialism of the State, there will no longer be a place within us for collective memory. And the word *Jew*, from Abraham to Dayan will come to represent, along with all the rest, just one kind of citizenship among many.

8

The Resurrection of
the Octopus

*I spent twenty years of my life in a country whose official ideology,
when confronted with any human problem, was always to reduce it
to a political phenomenon. (This ideological passion for the reduc-
tion of man is the evil that those coming from "back there" have
learned to despise the most.)* – Milan Kundera

Since the tragedy of Hitler, political anti-Semitism has all but
disappeared from the face of the earth. Not, of course, that
any magic spell suddenly stopped people from hating Jews.
But the ill will remains in an unfocused state. Prejudice
doesn't claim to be a worldview. What's needed for it to reach
the next level? Fear. The Nazis feared the Jews. So did Drumont and Dostoyevsky. Fear made Jews seem organized and
ubiquitous, and in possession of extraordinary powers. For
these political minds, Jews were not just foreigners with suspicious customs, but a superior adversary to be fought without mercy. "It is impossible to exaggerate the formidable stature of the Jew as enemy" (Hitler).

The Jews then offered a *demonstration of their powerlessness*
that lasted five years. You can still hate them, avoid contact
with them or distrust their chicanery. But there's no longer
any way to accord them the dignity of evil conspirators, seek-

147

ing to seize control of the world for themselves. You can't kill the devil; if you do, it's no longer the devil.

Even so, racist ideology couldn't keep its hands off the wreckage of Nazism. Universally rejected in public, it now shows its face only in private, with a violence that's frightening nonetheless. We've become used to this dichotomy: while politicians speak the language of justice and equality, it's left to individuals to express their brutal antipathies or racial prejudice. You can count on it: many racists wouldn't like it a bit if their ministers and representatives began making public use of the words they use in private. They'd be sincerely shocked by this sudden breach of decorum in political discourse, the intrusion of a violence and contempt that had no business there. It's as if the postwar period had decreed a divorce between politics and racism, and that modern morality works within each of us to make sure we respect this compulsory split.

As a result, hostility against the Jews can no longer be turned to political advantage. The name *Jew* itself gets in the way, designating them as an ethnic group that has suffered. That's why the word *Zionism* has become so important. Zionists need not be considered as members of a nation or race, but as partisan advocates of a system. The historical past doesn't prevent us from criticizing the harm that system has done, from exaggerating the power of its leaders, or keep us from according them the grand stature of mysterious, omnipotent characters who manipulate public opinion and determine the course of world events. Ideological anti-Semitism would hardly be able to flourish without christening itself anew, which it did, for the substitution of *Zionist* for *Jew* is more than just a rhetorical device. What it reveals is the mutation that totalitarian thought has undergone. In our era, we persecute ideologies, not whole peoples: there are no more subhuman species, just the henchmen of imperialism, fascists hiding behind the shield of the blue star of David, militants, and, in the last analysis, "a new kind of Nazism."[1] In short, racism can only be mentioned in contemporary political discourse under the sign of its opposite.

"ZIONIST!" GENEALOGY OF AN ACCUSATION

It was in the Paris of 1895 that Theodor Herzl conceived the idea of a Jewish state. "In his capacity as a correspondent, he had witnessed the public degradation of Alfred Dreyfus, and had seen the epaulets torn from this man who cried out: 'I'm innocent.' It was at that same moment that he became convinced in the depths of his soul that Dreyfus was innocent, and that he was only subject to this abominable suspicion because he was Jewish."[2] For Herzl, the Dreyfus Affair was proof that the entire assimilationist experience was in vain. The power of Reason was not up to the task of vanquishing anti-Semitism, that scourge of backward nations and ineradicable affliction of the most civilized. Jews would finally be left in peace only when they were at home in a land of their own. Was the solution a dream? Far less a dream, Herzl thought, than the unfulfilled hope of gaining full acceptance as citizens of other nations. The territorial idea, at least, was more than a dream, it was a utopia in the literal sense: a *place* for the Jews. Once people got over their astonished disbelief, the geographical solution was sure to please all sides. The Jews would gain security and respect, while the Others would be relieved of the intolerable presence of this foreign body. "They'll have to find us a bit of land on the surface of the globe: *an international ghetto*. . . . They can't throw all of us into the water, or at least can't burn us all alive."[3]

There were the two sides of Zionism: the lofty ideal of a Jewish state, and the willing agreement to become a world ghetto. The homeland Herzl hoped for was to be a land of spectacular *progress,* granting a millenial nation all the political prerogatives of modernity. But it was at the same time a kind of *throwback,* once again offering the Jews a life apart. Pride and disenchantment: Herzl flattered himself that this dual sentiment gave him a privileged lucidity that other theorists lacked. He saw the gentiles for what they were, instead of judging them by the ideals they professed.

All for naught! Anti-Semites would not be moved by this bitter realism, and the founding father would be given no credit for his hope of assembling the Jews in a particular place. The best example was the appearance at the turn of this century of the famous *Protocols of the Elders of Zion,* those apocryphal lectures in which a member of the secret Jewish government is supposed to have laid bare plans for seizing world control. The first editors of the text had designated the Alliance Israélite Universelle as the headquarters of this Freemasonry. Several years later (1905), the headquarters of Zion is moved, and it is in Bale, they assure us, in the halls of the First World Zionist Congress that the shady meeting of the Exilarques took place. From its very advent, or almost, the word *Zionist* would move beyond the control of its proponents and follow two divergent and separate courses, one in the Jewish community and the other in anti-Semitic discourse. What for Herzl and his people signified desire for a land and a state would be immediately interpreted by *the other side* as a conspiracy on a planetary scale, "which has the task of uniting all the Jews in the whole world in one union – a union which is more closely knit and more dangerous than the Jesuits."[4] Separatism is inverted into a tentacular plot; the initiative that should have, by all logic, shattered anti-Jewish propaganda instead feeds it and makes it more intense.

The Nazis would put this delirium to powerful effect. No hypocrites they, ferocity would become their philosophy. At once anti-Jewish and anti-Zionist, they would castigate Jews for a life that consisted of nothing but vampiristically preying on other nations, and Zionists – those generic enemies of the

State – for plotting the world's demise. A parasitic people can produce nothing but a politics of destruction. Barrès was already calmly declaring: "I conclude by his race that Dreyfus is capable of treason." In similar fashion, Hitler's metaphysics sees the Zionist conspiracy as springing from the Jewish instinct and going on to become its end result and perfect expression. As super-Jewish Jews, if I can dare to use such an expression, Zionists were pure products of their ethnic background (of their "species," as fascist terminology would put it), the most accomplished of Shem's children. Superior skill enabled them to conceal their voracious imperialism behind the harmless front seeking a state (Ha! a state on that arid, malaria infested land!).

Today, such logic persists only in an attenuated, residual form. The last world war shattered the causal link between the fated character of the Jewish people, the will to conquest and the subversion attributed to Zionism. The argument that every Jew must be a Zionist is now rarely heard, for the conscience of nations and the rhetoric of states today sees Hitlerism as the incarnation of evil. The people's republics and Arab countries condemn Israel's actions and the exorbitant power of its supporters, but without claiming them to be biological facts. Zionism can no longer be explained as an inexorable consequence of genetic law. It's become an independent entity, simultaneously an effect and its cause, a fault as well as its explanation, self-sustaining and powerful in itself. Though the expression "international Judaism" may crop up from time to time in some publication or other, there's no need to cry out at this telling *lapse*. It's now no more than what we call "a slip" in the midst of otherwise well-policed language: a reprehensible word, whose fault rests solely with the zealous individual who wrote or spoke it, not with the untarnished cause it is supposed to serve.

The postfascist age no longer thinks in terms of evil races or natural subversives, only of vile rhetoric and bad behavior; we fight against practices, not against nations, as we did in the savage outbreaks that marked this century's first half. As such, this might be considered moral progress when all is said and done: isn't it a comforting sight to see humanity linking arms in the fight for the power of fact and standing up for biological phantoms of old? Shouldn't such political independence be applauded?

And a specious maturity it is. New-look anti-Zionists vehemently deny any part of the Hitlerian legacy, while their black lyricism describes them as besieged by Zionists with a talent that would have made Rosenberg proud, the court philosopher of the Reich. The Enemy is still that thing of darkness, the political dracula who flees the light of day.

Whether he resides in the Third World or sits on some board of directors, whether he prefers banks and their comfortable surroundings or the tougher world of espionage, whether he's the gray eminence as chief of state or a media mogul, the Zionist is the man who works in the shadows cutting his underhanded deals. His objectives: it would be naive to assume they concerned the Jewish state alone. Israel is merely a piece of the puzzle, the first step in a strategy of world domination that Zionism and imperialism jointly undertake.

> Zionism, with its inhumane ethnic, racist principles, with its devilish schemes which generate chaos all over the world, with its dangerous plans to dominate, with its disregard for the appeals and resolutions of international organizations, and with its beastly octopus which has almost a decisive role in directing the policies of the greatest countries in the world, cannot be viewed as a threat to this region alone, but to the whole world.[5]

Who can say where its borders lie? Who will decide whether a Jew is innocent or part of the invisible empire, and by what criteria? What fraction of the people of Moses are loyal enough, pure enough to escape the suspicion of being Zionist? Especially when the image of the Zionist in the eyes of his detractors makes him a kind of infiltrating presence, with no fixed address or consistent rhetoric. You can't just look under "conspirators" in the Yellow Pages. Anti-Zionism is one of those frightening ideologies that rob their victims of the power to prove themselves innocent: the crime takes on an irrefutable existence as soon as someone is charged. The judge is all-powerful, capable of turning even the strongest argument for innocence into a crushing indictment. "You've never expressed openly Zionist opinions? That's because Zionism is a secretive undertaking, and you needed a cover." The court thus decides who is a Jew and who is a Zionist according to criteria available to it alone. If circumstances demand it, the condemnation can be extended to cover the whole range of Israelites, granting no one the status of *attenuated Jewishness*. Thus, without the least allusion to racism, all Jews find themselves guilty.

And it's much easier today than before the war to describe Zionism in the broadest possible terms. Until 1948, visionary exponents of the Jewish state were a minority within their communities. As we've seen, Bundists, communists, the religious and liberals alike all subjected them to merciless attacks. Those were the lean years, when anti-Semites had to use every sophistic talent at their disposal to prove that differences in the Jewish community were illusory, and that their quarrels were really a ploy to hoodwink the world. Anti-Zionists no longer need to perform such sleights of hand to make their case. Today, most Jews show some concern for the state of Israel. The feeling comes in many forms, and is expressed in an infinite number of ways: activism, financial support, emotional solidarity, a special curiosity about the news from Jerusalem. All that's required to transform the entire community into a secret society or a Cosa Nostra is to subsume all these differences under a single name: Zionism.

There is no more satisfying theory than a conspiracy theory. No sooner has it been adopted than all obstacles vanish, and the reality principle, that spoilsport, draws its last breath. It's the discourse that never fails: to believe in a conspiracy is to find shelter from reality. "The evidence is against me? I can't prove what I claim? If I could, it would only be a sign of weakness in my invincible enemy. In other words, who's tampering with the evidence? Who whips public opinion into a fury? Who distorts events? Who if not exactly that slippery octopus I so anxiously and untiringly denounce?" Such is the seduction of conspiracy: by turning every counterargument into additional evidence for its case, it offers its faithful a perfect, adamantine, unsubvertible system.

> While the name of Goebbels remains in the memory of man as the very symbol of successful propaganda, the irony of history has it that his victims, or rather those who claim to have been his victims on the strength of other people's corpses, should have become his spiritual heirs. They have spun a remarkable spider's web around the world and their capital, Tel Aviv, is a formidable centre for the transmission of propaganda, relayed by the mass media and diplomacy of Imperialism; by such means they have had considerable success in hoodwinking world public opinion.[6]

Zionist: the usefulness of the term couldn't escape Stalin, that grand master of the language of persecution. Let's give credit where credit is due: it was the contribution of this little leader of men to have launched the first anti-Zionist campaign of the post-Holocaust era. Of course, it didn't go off without a few glitches. At first, top billing in the Stalinist lexicon was given to the term *cosmopolitanism*. By evoking the down side of internationalism, the term was a useful way of charging people with an unprovable offense, and for depriving Jews of even the use of their name. Was he Jewish, Salomon Mikhoels, beaten to death in the streets of Minsk by agents of the Soviet police, April 13, 1948? Were they Jewish, the four hundred odd writers and artists who were liquidated as the fifties began? Were they Jewish, those Yiddish publications that were brutally banned, or the schools of Vilna and Kovo closed by the authorities? These claims were nothing but slander. Modern totalitarianism has nothing to do with oppressing the Jews; these were people and institutions punished for the crime of being cosmopolitan, not for their religion.

But the system had a flaw: the disparity between the flimsiness of the charges and the violence of the repression was simply too great. Cosmopolitans were surely deviants, as parasites and as exiles. But working for whom? The word evokes a kind of treason, not a conspiracy; it isn't quite enough to justify persecution. *Zionism* would be the term that would cover this slight deficit in the moral account. Thanks to close relations between Israel and the United States, from now on the domestic enemy would no longer be an assortment of shady individuals but a highly organized and active coalition. The cosmopolitan was a suspect; the Zionist was guilty as charged. The cosmopolitan loved neither his country nor socialism: the Zionist was a member of a secret organization that worked night and day to subvert them. It was a label worthy of the kind of purge Stalin had in mind. In the name of anti-Zionism, all was permitted. The Doctor's Plot in Moscow. The Slansky trial in Prague. Ten doctors wanting to kill the good Georgian; fifteen dignitaries of the Czech Communist Party as suspected CIA agents. Everything was possible once the concept of Zionism was put into play.

Today's anti-Zionism has no original material: everything is a refinement on Comrade Stalin's brilliant innovations. No more scapegoats are required, just political enemies; no need for a cultural enemy, just the division of the world into rival camps; no more Jews, just Zionists, those fomenters of both a noxious ideology and unsettling conspiracy. Stalin can be proud of his children: thirty years of research and effort have brought the Zionist conspiracy from the era of piecework into the industrial mode of production. By using the most vehement diatribes available today, anti-Zionism has almost erased the distinction between the puppet and puppetmaster pulling the strings: maybe the Zionists are directing U.S. imperialism, maybe the Pentagon has already fallen into their hands. As for the ideology itself, we remember the famous UN resolution that, on November 10, 1975, defined Zionism as a form of racism. Anti-Zionism thus struck a double blow: it gained international recognition, hitting the mark by projecting its own fault onto the prey it attacked. The condemnation of the Jews for racism was Stalin's greatest posthumous success, an unbelievable joke, with modern totalitarianism unable to contain its laughter.[7]

And the same analysis holds for the Arab countries as well. It's certainly true that they aren't part of the common Judeophobic tradition kept alive by Russia and Poland, and that they don't have genocide on their conscience as Europe does. But it's also the case that they have reasons of their own to resist the Israeli presence. Every historical instance of settling a new population on already occupied territory has brought problems in its wake. In choosing nevertheless to call their adversaries the "Zionist entity," these states have turned the Arab-Israeli conflict into an avatar of the Jewish Question. The concept of Zionism cancels all nuances, suppresses distinctions, and abolishes differences of degree: it conceives of an opponent comprised of civilians and soldiers, sympathizers and activists, the Diaspora and the state of Israel. Every Jew, wherever he lives and whatever he does, can appear as an enemy. The Israeli out of uniform and the most peace-loving

Israelite discover themselves to be unwitting soldiers of a gigantic secret army, through a doctrine that places the entire Jewish people under the double banner of Israeli expansionism and world reaction.

Anti-Zionism wages its war only against combatants. It's a nice idea, but with one slight problem: the anti-Zionist worldview has no room for noncombatants. What good does it do, on the one hand, to *politicize* the issues, if on the other you refuse to place any bounds on the political sphere? What good does it do to delimit your enemy (the Zionist, and no one else) and the grounds for your hostility (imperialism, colonialism), when elsewhere you paint the crime of Zionism with such broad strokes that practically any Jew is guilty as charged? Such generalized hatred gives every appearance of being a limited form of opposition. Terrorism is a direct consequence of this distortion. If there are no longer any innocents, only a "Zionist entity," any random attack will always be a direct hit, and the most aleatory violence is already justified.

The Left, at least a certain Left, is repelled by the thought that there might be Arab anti-Semitism. Anyone who ventures this hypothesis is immediately accused of defamation. Three arguments, always the same, are cited as proof: since the Arabs are Semites themselves, how can they be accused of anti-Semitism? Before the disastrous creation of Israel, relations between Islam and the Jewish communities living at its heart had always been excellent. The Jewish state, finally, would never have been born if the war hadn't made the West feel the need to compensate its victims: Europe salved its guilty conscience by committing a new injustice, this time against the Arabs. This three-pronged argument deserves further examination, if only for the favor it finds among progressives of all countries, and for the wonderful and promising ideological future it holds.

You don't saw off the branch you're sitting on: Semites

can't be anti-Semitic. A superb syllogism, but one that doesn't take this into account: *anti-Semitism* is a recent word. Invented around 1850 by a certain Wilhelm Marr, the term has never had any other purpose than dressing up anti-Jewish sentiment as a field of scholarly research in the Humanities, as something crucial in the struggle for survival. It is Jews and no one else who continue to be hated. Rebaptized as Semites, they're no longer a religion but transformed into a race. The change signaled the passage from inquisition to an all-out war. Properly speaking, Western anti-Semitism thus has no more existence than does Arab anti-Semitism: what appears to be anti-Semitism is never anything but the scientifically certified ethnocidal variant that is anti-Jewish prejudice.

As for relations between Moslems and Jews, they were less idyllic than the picture that kindhearted propaganda would like to paint. The Jews were "dhimmis," a protectorate of Islam. As such, they had to pay a special tax and lavish tokens of respect and deference on the True Believers. From this arose the necessity of everything from wearing a distinctive symbol to a ban on building houses that were taller than a Moslem's, or on touching a Moslem woman. To be sure, the Jews enjoyed a relative security that their European coreligionists might have envied. There was never any attempt to force them to accept the Islamic faith, and they were never deported (before the creation of Israel) from any Arab country. They were nevertheless subject to a persecution that ranged from individual humiliation to pogroms. To those nostalgic for a would-be Judeo-Arabic golden age, Albert Memmi usefully recalls the most recent examples: 1907: massacre in Casablanca; 1912: the great massacre in Fez; 1936: the massacre of Constantine, 24 dead, scores of seriously wounded; 1945: massacre in Tripoli, and more.[8]

An essential distinction remains, however, between European anti-Semitism and the contempt in which Islam traditionally held the people of the Book. Eastern Jews were considered a *weak minority,* and Moslem polemics held this political inferiority to be proof of religious inferiority. While Christianity and later the secular West believed in the myth of Jewish power, Islam took the opposite course and chose to emphasize Jewish poverty and impotence. Mohammed had brought forth Islam: the miracle attested to its divine mission. In short, it is not anti-Judaism as such that has been characteristic of the West up into the present, but rather the *exterminatory* wish behind anti-Jewish feeling: a frightening, apocalyptic hatred that depicts the Jews as "so overwhelmingly powerful that the only way to cope with them is to destroy them utterly."[9]

It took the appearance of the Jewish state for Western anti-Semitic discourse to penetrate Islam. Israel, as they still say in most Arab countries, is an American enclave, a thorn, a wound, a festering scar on the body of the Arab (or Islamic) nation. But metaphors don't account for the full extent of Western influence. Anti-Semitism was brought to Arab soil disguised as antipathy toward Israel as a Western country. In violent attacks against Israeli usurpation, radical Arabs don't restrict themselves to the language of law. Denunciations of the worldwide Zionist conspiracy accompanies the legal claim for Palestinian territory. The mellahs swarming with a poor and humble populace are gone, and the hour of the Zionists – with their arrogant array of endless schemes – has come. The enemy is no longer the dhimmi, an inferior subaltern whom one could treat, according to whim, with benevolence or disdain: he is now the collective incarnation of evil and conspires to ruin the human race. With this change in its image of the Jew, Islam has joined the ranks of European anti-Semitism. For its own tradition was literally impoverished in comparison with the arsenal of accusations which Marxist and Christian culture had in store. It's an ideology that travels well and is quickly learned, and to judge by several recent publications, the student has done his teacher proud.[10] Who, after all, is the first postwar head of state to make himself a *public* apologist for the *Protocols of the Elders of Zion*? Nasser, the hero of Third Worldism.[11] This forgery, already extensively circulated since its promotion by czarist Russia, still has a lot of shelf life left: after the defection ("the betrayal") of Egypt, it continues to be a reference work in all the countries on the Rejectionist Front. Hatred of the West, whose current mainstay is Zionism, resounds with echoes strangely familiar to Western memory.

The pioneers of the back-to-Zion movement had but a single desire: to gather the Jews and put an end to two thousand years of scattering and exile. Their hope has certainly gone unfulfilled, all the more so in their inability to make themselves understood. Today, old fears of the Jewish Diaspora ironically return in the guise of anti-Zionism. In fact, what fosters this rhetoric and provides its apocalyptic hue is not the massing of the Jews in a single place, but its opposite: their dispersal to the four corners of the earth. The minuscule Jewish state is, in the eyes of its enemies, the agent of a colossal, clandestine organization, "the capital of an elusive and omnipresent empire" wrote Philippe de Saint-Robert in the pages of *Le Monde*.[12] The Jewish people make up, including Israel, an extensive but cohesive network of communities; anti-Zionism grounds its fundamental argument on this intolerable absurdity. What do these people scattered throughout the planet do? Hovering in the shadows, they connive to bring about the demise of the Good. What common bond brings them together across the babel of languages and disparate ways of life? Conspiracy, that unbreakable link. *Diaspora = Mafia:* the sinister notion of a Jewish plot was born of this equation, and the same image, unchanged in everything but vocabulary, provides the basis for contemporary anti-Zionism.

Maurras once made this shattering admission in confidence: "It all seems impossible or frightfully difficult, without the providence of anti-Semitism. Through it, everything works, becomes clear and simple. If you weren't an anti-Semite out of patriotism, you'd become one out of sheer opportunism." It's nice, in fact, to have an enemy who's both invisible and all-powerful: it gives you a feeling of complete clarity and irresponsibility. Everything's the fault of the Other, the Grand Antagonist; there's nothing, absolutely nothing for which he can't answer, and you're exempt in advance from any further inquiry. Anti-Semitism guarantees the double pleasure of definitive clarity intellectually and perfect innocence morally. For those who wage war against him, the Zionist is a similar blessing: so demoniacal as a subterranean adversary, so widespread, so organized, so *diasporic* that you can attribute any evil act to him without risking incoherence. When the Syrian army bombed the Palestinian camp of Tall-El-Zaatar into oblivion in 1976, the Franco-Palestinian Medical Association published, with complete self-assurance, the following declaration:

> The Assad Government . . . is today the main agent of imperialist and Zionist plots designed to encompass the destruction of the Palestinian resistance movement.[13]

But the record-holder in this event seems to be the Islamic republic of the Imam Khomeni. There's no defeat, no failure, no difficulty, no opponent in which the leaders of the Iranian revolution haven't discovered a Zionist hand. If one were to believe the allegations of the new regime, Zionists probably control the wire services, must have been implicated in the Kurdish uprising, dictate the politics of the American Senate and were probably the poisoners of the Ayatollah Taleghani. Quite a bit for a single adversary, but far-flung and invisible Zionists are not just any enemy. With the Diaspora, you've got to be ready for anything. Zionists can turn up everywhere at once, in defiance of all logic: you've got to be on the lookout for that incomparable empress of evil, more wicked than America, Hitler and all the incarnations of Satan rolled up into one.

Emigrés from the East Block have often made the ironic and bitter observation that dogma is mouthed only in those countries where it remains out of power. A petrified Marxism still claims its functionaries and victims in the peoples' republics, while liberal Europe is where its advocates and militant backers are to be found. No Western country considers Zionism to be a crime, but the word *Zionist* is sometimes used as an insult. What for the East is a criminal category is for us a living concept. The unique contribution of Western Marxism has been its revival of dead languages: a red cap has been placed atop the criminal code, and worn-out slogans refreshed with a new revolutionary fervor.

Many of us, in any case, have paid the price. As young Jews aching to belong to a people crowned by sorrow, we couldn't wait for someone to treat us like a "kike." We imagined how we'd respond, and looked forward to smashing him. But instead of a thug, a superpatriot or a little Nazi, we were confronted wherever we turned by would-be instructors and preening pros of good conscience, ready to give us a few tips. They held our racism but not our race against us, saw us as the tools of a theocratic, imperialist and militaristic state, and hated us for being colonizers and paras, not exiles or nomads.[14] Having ceased to be a persecuted minority and become the arrogant oppressors, we were given but a single chance of reclaiming our previous image: produce our certificate of divorce from Israel. An inquisitorial atmosphere dominated progressive circles of the period. To be accepted as a Jew, all ties with Zionism had to be cut, just as in the past, liberal France conferred the status of Israelite on those of the Prophet's descendants who no longer retained the slightest trace of Jewishness. The position of the Jew had undergone a reversal, and the rules of the game had changed. What hadn't, to put it boldly, was the demand to come clean, the obligation to answer before the bar.

Whether Zionist or Jew, the revolution brooked no compromise, complexity or partial gestures. It was well understood that we would be held responsible for the most minute trace of toleration toward Israel, and that demonstrating any concern for its survival would forever place us on the executioners' side. And this was the more indulgent position; hardcore militants had purged the word *Jew* from their vocabulary. All was political and everything had to be decided on the spot. Activists looked to history only for emblems or metaphors that might be useful in the present, entering it like a wardrobe and removing only the events and personages they could use. Let the petit bourgeois, the aesthetes and the idle burnish their memories and burden themselves with needless nightmares. Those who lived in a state of emergency had no time to waste keeping up monuments to the dead. Never look back, never count past two: these were the basic laws governing their behavior. Neither memory nor nuances could be allowed to get in action's way. Workers/bosses; socialism/barbarism; imperialism/Third World; Zionists/Palestinians: such structural oppositions magically opened the gates of the palace of wisdom. How could they be charged with anti-Semitism, when a world without Jews unfolded before their eyes?

This activism has lost much of its power to intimidate, but has become more radical among its few remaining practitioners. On March 27, 1979, at lunchtime, a bomb exploded in front of the Israelite university restaurant on the Rue Médicis in Paris. The attack left twenty-six wounded, two seriously. Miraculously no one died. The police (is anyone surprised?) didn't find the perpetrators. What we know of their motives comes from the name they gave: "Autonomous collective of intervention against the Zionist presence in France and against the Israeli-Egyptian peace treaty." A phony lead to throw us off the track? I think not: their delirious terminology should be taken at its word. The terrorists felt they had a mandate. They made war, and didn't strike randomly at civilians but at a *hotbed of Zionists,* a stronghold in the enemy camp. This transformation of politics into a holy war became an absolute politicization of the real; the logic of anti-Zionism had been applied with absolute rigor, and turned into a death machine.

There's but one lesson to be learned from this attack: *the Jew is absent from anti-Semitism in its murderous form.* He for whom the Jews exist will not be the one to kill them: memory at least keeps him from making the move from prejudice to physical attack. For radical anti-Zionists, the Jew does not exist. Unburdened by scruples, and without memory to temper his zeal, he hasn't the slightest notion of what anti-Semitism might be and thus reproduces its horror. As a sincere militant, he isn't one to hide visceral hatred beneath a duplicitous or clever mask. Anti-Zionism is not a style he affects, and there's no limiting principle to its violence. He's protected from doubt and remorse, for the new enemy to be fought is the symbol of every quality the political morality of the last half-century has taught him to hate: racism, imperialism, the supremacy of money. So he commits himself to the cause with the *energy of innocence.* And it's the most frightening kind of innocence: forgetfulness itself. History would never repeat itself if its actors didn't occasionally assume the terrible self-certainty of defending a pure and wholly original cause.

ARGUMENT FOR THE UNDETERMINABLE

Anti-Semitism sometimes changes its name, but never its story. It always tells the same dark tale of intrigue and conspiracy. Whether Zionist or Jew, the anti-hero of the tale possesses the same powers: those of the *octopus,* that multiplex creature ensnaring a mighty count of victims in its tentacles, possessing the powers of a *spider* patiently weaving its invisible web, enclosing or hoping to enclose the entire human race in its network's coils. It's a picture of the Jew as insect or cephalopod. But why these beasts in particular? Why does the antipathy toward Jews systematically take the form of paranoia? No doubt because the foreignness of Jews is a kind of difference *unlike others*. They are "those people" whom no label fits, whether assigned by the Gaze, the Concept or the State. There is, to be sure, a Jewish type, but the rule has too many exceptions to be a reliable guide. Or rather for Jewishness, the type is the exception and its absence is the rule: in fact, you can rarely pick out a Jew at first glance. It's an insubstantial difference that resists definition as much as it frustrates the eye: are they a people? a religion? a nation? All these categories apply, but none is adequate in itself. The Jews are to be found everywhere. Since the breakup of the ghettos, they can't be localized in a single group. Diaspora, invisibility, indeterminacy: it's this triple failure of clarity that makes Jews so vulnerable to accusations of conspiracy. A trifle suffices to make the image seem real, some nothing that transforms historical opacity into *intentional* mystery, triggering the barely perceptible slippage that turns a "problem people" (J. P. Faye) into an occult sect. You can't recognize a Jew when you see one? It's part and parcel of his secretive nature. He's not easily defined? It's because he pursues unspeakable goals. And "if he is scattered all over the world, it's because all the world must belong to him."[15]

As we've seen, it's always consoling to explain our frustrations as the result of a single cause, to discover a clandestine order beneath the chaos of the world, even if that order is an abomination. The conspiracy theme is a pleasing idea. And the Jew, that elusive Other, is the best possible devil for our secular world. If he were just a foreigner, anti-Semitism – a variant of racism – would be content to reject him or keep him at arm's length. But of all possible mongrels it's the Jew alone (or, after Auschwitz, the Zionist) who fits the bill as the Grand Enemy. This is what makes anti-Semitism unique.

The Jews have thus been afflicted with a mystery that they've done everything possible to diminish over the past two centuries. Assimilation, then Zionism shared the common aim of making the fact of one's Jewishness into something of trivial significance. "We're a religion," the liberals would declare, meaning a private faith like Catholicism. "We're a nation," partisan supporters of the return to the land of the Patriarchs would exclaim, "a nation in which we will be full citizens, just like the Poles in Poland and the French in France, in a nation which is legally ours." The two projects were bound to conflict, since one advocated the individual's assimilation while the other laid claim to "that model of social organization – the nation-state – through which other peoples guaranteed their security and way of life."[16] But the basic procedure was the same. In each case it was a question of making the complex simple, of changing a muddy picture to one of perfect clarity. What Zionists and the backers of integration each wanted in their own way was for Judaism to put an end to its undecidability and become a categorizable difference. Whether as a religion or nation, their otherness would acquire the definitive quality of a comprehensible attribute, and cease being a dark continent onto which everything possible could be projected. *The case would be closed.*

False hopes. Today we live in the post-Zionist but also the post-assimilationist era, and the situation is *less clear than ever*. The need to give the word *Jew* an unequivocal and precise content remains an unfulfilled dream, and is hardly to be achieved through an act of intellectual will. "May there be neither Jews nor Christians unless it be at the moment of prayer for those who pray"— such was the ideal that the philosophy of the Enlightenment set before the Jews. Modernity itself has its origins in this principle. Neither Jews nor Christians, in fact, would exist in the sense that all visible signs of their difference from one another were supposed to have been erased. But in spite of everything, Jewishness has refused to confine itself to the sphere of religious life. Jews who are atheists or assimilated enough to be indistinguishable from their neighbors persist and continue to remain Jewish, even when they have little idea what their obstinacy means. What is this religion that isn't one and makes its claims felt on the unbelievers? What meaning can the noun *Jew* carry when it no longer signifies a faith or affiliation? Instead of being resolved, the enigma has become darker yet. And Zionism's success hasn't changed the equation: the Diaspora has demonstrated loyalty to Israel as well as its own wish for survival. Solidarity, at least, has taken every form save that of emigration. The Jews have a kingdom they want to support without necessarily moving there themselves. In short, the realization of Zionism has only added the dimension of statehood to the Jewish experience, without suppressing its other components. Jewishness is no more determined by its national definition than by its places of worship or liturgical practice.

And so when Jacques Frémontier asserts: "I think that Israel renders an immense service to French Jews: either one feels Jewish, and goes there; or one doesn't feel Jewish and instead stays here"[17]— the author of *Worker Stronghold* mistakes, as they say, his desire for reality. The former communist militant has kept up the sharp totalitarian reflexes he acquired during his time in the PC (French Communist Party), especially the penchant for reductionism that Kundera describes: everything must be political, with no exceptions made. Aspects of real experience that *can't be included* are voided and legislated out of existence. As Frémontier puts it, there's exactly nothing between French and Israeli citizenship. The construction of such a peremptory analysis works as a kind of hypnotic self-suggestion, serving to dismiss uncertainty and to keep it at bay. For a certain nostalgia lurks beneath the apparent brutality of Frémontier's words. While the state of Israel has helped the Jews of France in ways that are undeniable, it hasn't succeeded in making their situation any simpler: neither Zionism nor assimilation can claim to have *settled* the Jewish question. For a final resolution would be undesirable. Something unfinished is at work in contemporary Jewry, something impure and bastardized – a deafness that refuses enlightenment, and a stubborn refusal to let itself be encompassed by a stable and recognized concept. To those of us schooled in the categories of class, state and religion, such pushcart Jewishness – borrowing from each of these notions without fitting any one of them – can appear to be a kind of defiance or extravagant opacity. Our identity *doesn't ring true:* it's out of tune with the words we speak. Nothing could be more natural, it seems, than to want to bring our identity into harmony with the rest and mold the person to fit the system. "Let's be Jewish, but according to some aesthetic rule, respecting the different versions that comprise it, instead of dragging an aura of the unthinkable and the absurd around with us wherever we go. . ."

But there's no need to rush and cave in to this temptation. To nationalize Judaism, or better yet, to make it a church, is to arrest it, in the sense of freezing a changing process or interrogating a smuggler who makes cross-border runs. It is thus to make Judaism subject, under the pretext of bringing our life and discourse into harmony, to the police state and its regime. Restrict the word *Jew* to a single truth and there we are: suddenly capable of judging, categorizing, classifying and finally diminishing those who don't conform to our idea of our common bond. Several Jewish thinkers have begun to practice such small-time terror under the lofty banner of the renewal of

Judaism. Shmuel Trigano, for example, when he thinks he's unmasking Yiddishkeit as a corruption of original Judaism. Or take Annie Kriegel, when in the name of solidarity with Israel she crusades against "the mysterious virtues of nostalgia for Yiddishkeit," for the "Sephardic path of the future."[18] There are no phony Jews: there are only authentic inquisitors. No defense will ever be strong enough against the desire to establish orthodoxy, against the desire to make life simple.

We Jews are certainly too busy bustling here and there to nail down a *definition* of what this collective sensibility means. For the prejudiced, such a "we" has only one meaning, the spirit of clan, cabal or conspiracy. The "we" of collaboration and shady plots. The arachnian "we" of a secret coterie that promotes its interests by illicit means. The Jewish response to such monstrous accusations has traditionally been to deny all solidarity. There is no "we," they declared, for Judaism is a private affair. Today they dare once more to risk affirming themselves as a community. And just as quickly, certain among them push to normalize this "we," to give it a statist and national content. But why must collective expression always remain the exclusive province of politics? Why would anything that is not "I" necessarily be a question of power or of state? Judaism's very lack of definition is precious: it shows that political categories of class or of nation have only a relative truth, and stands as a sign of their inability to encompass the world in its totality. The Jewish people don't know what they are, only that they exist, and that their disconcerting existence blurs the boundary, inaugurated by modern reason, between the public and the private.

9
Another Desire

The independent subject is unseated by a wordless accusation.
— Emmanuel Lévinas

For the longest time, all that I have retained of Judaism has
been the adjective it accorded me and the narcissistic use I
made of it. Jew: as in Just, Exile, Victim, Rebellious People,
The Vale of Tears . . . My discretion and efficiency were invincible in the handling of these connotations. They sketched the
self-image I hoped to suggest to other men, and made my life
the cynosure of an enchanted circle. A Jew just for show? Not
exactly, for I didn't disguise but unveiled myself, offered the
precious secret of my personality to public view. But I was also
seeking, in the interest provoked by my self-revelation, proof
that I wasn't just anyone. While it sounded like a proclamation, in fact I was asking my interlocutor for permission to exist. "It is sufficient that others look at me," said Sartre, "for me
to be what I am." The other side of such omnipotence is that it
is sufficient that others not look at me for me to cease existing
altogether: for the possessor of an orphaned self, a self without grounds, such an identity can become a trap. The Other
exercises a constitutive power when he points you out and an
annihilating power when, distracted or hurried, he *passes*
without giving you the benefit of the smallest glance. Until recently, literary honors went only to identifiable Jews, pinned
to their Jewishness by the violence of an alien word. Now,
what made me Jewish was not the gaze of the Other, but the

competitive desire to capture his attention for myself when it was being sought by everyone else. Was I alienated from the object I had become for the benefit of others? Hardly. I was in dread that I'd leave them with no lasting impression of who I was. I buttonholed passersby, so that they might witness the spectacle of my difference. As the consummate clown, I attracted the public in droves: "the Jew" was my most effective number, the most original material I had to offer. I was no liar or perjurer like those converts, the others who deserted Judaism, or those who assimilated. I simply played myself, jubilantly and stubbornly holding onto the juicy role of the pariah as if for life.

But this book is not the edifying tale of ascetic withdrawal or an inner moral journey. I didn't undertake it to recount the victory of my authentic self over its production. For there's finally no getting away from the stage: to say "I" is already to take a pose, perpetually to renew our mourning for the vain, seductive, voracious self that appropriates the history of an entire people and makes it part of the need to be loved.

I have not killed my image. Despite my efforts at reform and spiritual improvement, I have yet to banish the personal devil who plays Mr. Important the moment I speak of Jewish things. Finally, however, its presence makes little difference. For if being Jewish continues to be a way of making me desirable (or *remarkable,* which amounts to the same thing), such a mundane strategy no longer has the final word. Out of habit, for the secret pleasure, and because it is hardly possible for me to do otherwise, I still play on my difference, but I've come to understand that Judaism is not simply a matter of expression or of personal sincerity, that it's to be found outside myself and that it resists any definition in the *first person singular.* Gone are the days when I, consumed with passion for my own individuality, had nothing to learn from Judaism, as if I'd been born knowing everything about it I might need. I am therefore incapable of recounting, after so many others have done so, just how, by what miracle, through what trauma I became a Jew, for I've been one for as long as I can remember. The opposite question stands at the origin of this book: how Judaism, that land where I believed I was born, *came to be something I lacked.*

It is now clear to me that once my family disappears, I will never be able to bring that culture back to life to which I naively thought I was heir. In naive and dashing fashion, I slipped my Jewishness on like a custom-made suit until that day – belatedly – when I became aware that my parents wouldn't live forever. It was then, in fact, that the world they embodied no longer appeared as a *fact,* but as a *secret,* as an exclusive, perishable quality that I will forever be unable to possess. I know what I'm going to lose: and it's this newly acquired clarity that makes me the enemy of my own airs and that protests against the majesty of the Jew-King (His Majesty the Jew: our generation's fantasy, when it dreamt of the yellow star, the majesty of banishment and its sorrow).

An active memory stores up all that it can: fragments of a civilization that have survived exile, expressions and gestures to tell them with, a philosophy of life and frame of mind. But only to be the dupe of my own labors? How can I ignore that cultural spontaneity that I will always lack, or the fact that, whatever happens, I will miss what can't be replaced? My childhood, or at least the part spent outside school, steeped in "this atmosphere – so unique that it is difficult to give an idea of it to those who don't have direct experience of it – that immigrant Jews are able to make of their surroundings in the country of their second exile."[1] Whether religious or, as is my case, entirely secular, such an ambiance is already strongly diluted proof of a Judaism that lives, but which will not survive the generation that escaped the Holocaust. A family history? If you wish, but only to the extent that this family is neither a homogeneous site nor an Oedipal battleground, but a cultural space traversed by history, built of layers, as Deleuze would say, that are not familial at all.

So it was that throughout my interminable adolescence, I joined an obsession with my Jewish identity with absolute indifference towards Judaism. Achieving maturity was simply a matter of moving from plenitude to penury. A sense of my own originality has now been overshadowed by nostalgia for what I can never be. It's taken time, it's true, for the evidence to prevail, but I can plead extenuating circumstances: to not have been self-absorbed, I would have to have been courageous enough to swim against the tide. Everything encouraged my disdain for memory, and if I hadn't acceded to the general rule, a terrible indictment lay in store. I would have abandoned history and become that most despicable of creatures: a reactionary. Though our world was political through and through, from the top of its hat to the tips of its toes, Jewishness was to be defended only as a symbol, as something unspoken yet present in all forms of collective oppression. Everything else – its spiritual tradition, social history, daily life – didn't exist. The cultural dimension had no place in this vision of the world, effectively tossing out everything that was neither right nor left, all aspects of a civilization that weren't reducible to a *cause* or that didn't fit the framework of *combat*. For it's not to be forgotten that we are the offspring of an era that replaced the political as a separate sphere with politics as a boundless empire, an all-inclusive totality. Everything that was real was political; only things that were political were real. For us, there was no neutral ground; we were hardly so naive! We could unmask conflicts that roiled under the lies of a calm exterior, confrontations, could identify the power relations at work in the innumerable sites where power was exercised, and where resistance was to be mounted to counter its effects.

Down to the most subtle workings of social life, we had but a single concern: the struggle.

The Jew, exemplary victim of persecution, served as a point of reference. The assorted causes of the moment were likened to the sorrows of Jewish experience, as a way of gauging the extent of a given barbarity, coming up with a relative measure of oppressors and validating rebellions as well. For we belonged, and to some extent still belong, to the post-Hitler era. The Nazi era imprinted itself on us so strongly that we're unable to offer a definition of violence or evil that doesn't immediately evoke its image. There's not a single revolt or single struggle of the last forty years that hasn't borne the stamp of antifascism. From the battered woman to the immigrant worker, from the Chilean junta to the children of Cambodia and on to the prisoners of the gulag, each victim brings the Jew back to life. The swaggering profile of any oppressor casts the shadow of the Nazi executioner. The result: a split, a schism between the Jew in the abstract, who functioned as a kind of standard measure for comparing all types of misfortune, and the concrete Jew, neglected in favor of the *latest* victims. The one rose to the rank of oppression's showhorse while the other was relegated to the dustbin of history. In short, the Jew was useful as a measuring stick only if he was first stripped of his concrete, living character.

As a Jew on the Left, I passively reproduced this dissociation within myself. I affirmed my Jewishness in each of my political choices; I was politically active only as an identified Jew. But at the same time and for the same reason, I scorned Jewish culture, that distant folklore and febrile tradition that could only dilute the power of my militant stance. It was Judaism as a body of knowledge and history that suffered most from my overinvestment in the Jewish paradigm.

But the atmosphere that produced "Everything is political" has passed. Some miss those days when life was given a militant direction, when we set out to conquer the truth, armed only with the words *left* and *right*. I don't share their nostalgia. If the political had remained in control of our collective superego, I would have spent my entire life as a committed Jew, authentic and proud, without knowing a thing about the importance or even the reality of Judaism. A crisis of the political exists today: what's known as the Jewish renaissance or renewal is one of many consequences this aggravation has brought.

✡

What I have tried to tell here is the story of a leave-taking. Once, I loved myself through my Jewish identity, while today I love Judaism because I receive it from without, because it brings me more than I contain within. I was sated with my role, imbued with a pathetic and marvelous Jewish self that I adored as if it were an idol. I then underwent a strange experience: an undoing of the self and its idolatrous cult. Judaism, for me, is no longer a kind of identity as much as a kind of transcendence. Not something that defines me but a culture that can't be embraced, a grace I cannot claim as my own. In twenty years at the most, there will be no more than a handful of professional historians to tell us of the Jewish culture of Central Europe and of the genocide that brought it to an end. We occupy that pivotal moment, that detestable moment, when our past enters into history. The last survivors of this civilization disappear, turning it into a sort of vague and bygone era, abandoned by the general populace and snatched up by the specialists. The Judaism into which I was born is increasingly acquiring the status of a historical object, marked by a sudden distance making it both a painful and desirable object of reflection. Until recently, it had always let me experience my Jewishness, whereas now I experience it as an absence.

And anti-Semitism has played no part in this transformation, despite the rumblings of the last few months and the unreal atmosphere we've been made to inhabit. Without anything really going on, the worst seemed absolutely sure to occur. It was a time "buzzing with sinister forebodings."[2] A muckraking book published with great fanfare – only thinly veiled as investigative reporting – had sounded the alarm that, forty years later, France was about to become unlivable for Jews. Vichy was rising from the ashes, and collaborationist ghosts had returned to haunt our existence; we were consumed by fantastic possibilities, frantic with concern. Fascist writers on display in store windows, nostalgia at half-mast, retro hair styles and pleated pants on the terraces of chic cafés: the staging was set, and the beast could be seen everywhere, sticking his snout out from behind the curtains.

Here and there, a few voices were raised in dissent. Poliakov, the chronicler of twenty centuries of hatred, displayed his usual serenity, even seemed to excuse his optimism with a bit of understated humor: "In our time," he declared, "the two great bastions of thought and of intellectual growth, the Church and the University, are rigorously hostile toward any form of anti-Semitism. Such was not always the case before the Second World War."[3] As for Jankélévitch, he kept his distance from the "belated concern" of the "new crusaders who are discovering, today, that Jews have been a persecuted group."[4] People bowed before the authority of these two prestigious figures, but they didn't hear what they had to say. The leftist intelligentsia had better things to do. Now, after thirty years of almost total blindness, master and apprentice thinkers were surprised to discover – and grandiloquently let it be known – that anti-Semitism hadn't vanished with the horror of the camps. People had gotten used to the idea that the people of Israel were no longer vulnerable enough to merit the name they bore; the metaphor Jew was to be applied only to the revolutionary oppressed . . . And then, with help from a Marxism in crisis, the Jews rediscovered their right to a history and stopped being occulted, even condemned, by a symbol that was their own.

The turnabout was spectacular, but it wasn't enough to put a dent in the self-assured arrogance of our brilliant intelligentsia. Without the slightest hesitation, their changing positions on the issue became identified with the march of time. They certainly couldn't have been blind – that would be a sacrilegious charge to level against people whose job is to see beyond appearances. Their position hadn't changed, but history had, in a world in which suddenly the Jewish problem had become particularly acute. Oh joyful confusion: the indifferent of yesterday became today's prophets of doom, as the new resistance fighters were spared any need for modesty by playing to *current* anxiety. Time for a few best-sellers.

There would hardly be any reason to take offense at this artificial drama if it weren't so *seductive*. Many young Jews gave in to the temptation of bringing back to imaginary life what prior generations had experienced in reality. And for the first time, the world seemed to go along with their internal theater. Who could have hoped for such cooperation! It was difficult not to take advantage of the audience listening in, to become a publicist for your own misfortune, your emotional states and wounded sense of self. To be sure, you can't be too careful where anti-Semitism is concerned. But such attention runs the risk of regression if it gives love of Judaism only this single means of expression: the repetitive, pretentious and vain proclamation of our alterity.

For the hallowed right to be different hides an insidious constraint beneath its liberatory appearance: the obligation to conceive of Judaism in terms of self and identity. "I am a Jew," I declared, and this sentence distilled my knowledge of Judaism, my profound truth and my rediscovered dignity. The only language I spoke was one in which I made demands. I had taken up residence in defiance, and spent many happy days there. It was this imaginary encampment at the bounds of society – my obsession with posturing more than social pressure or the imperatives of assimilation – that kept me distant from Jewish culture. Now I expiate this narcissistic frenzy, reporting on Judaism as I have not lived it, spending time constructing the ghettos of Spain for myself. The word *Jew* is no longer a mirror in which I seek my self-portrait, but where I look for everything I'm not, everything I'll never be able to glimpse by taking myself as a point of reference. Thinking I was living on the margins, lecturing all who would listen about my uniqueness, I was seized by an agonizing realization as a wordless accusation made bombast seem disgusting: those who were the very inspiration of my Judaism were one day going to die. It was a disappearance I was unable to let my ignorance permit. A task was incumbent upon me, one in which the lyricism of the outcast had no part. Hysterical, I had been Jewish in order to be noticed; now I learned loyalty, and began the imperfect construction of a memory that would retain and transmit as much truth as possible about those beings who taught me that Judaism was something to love.

Notes

INTRODUCTION

1. For biographical information on Finkielkraut, see Judith Friedlander, *Vilna on the Seine: Jewish Intellectuals in France Since 1940.* (New Haven: Yale University Press, 1990).

2. See Alain Finkielkraut, *The Undoing of Thought,* trans. Dennis O'Keefe (London and Lexington: The Claridge Press, 1988), and *Remembering in Vain: The Klaus Barbie Trial and Crimes Against Humanity,* trans. Roxanne Lapidus with Sima Godfrey (New York: Columbia University Press, 1993).

3. See Arthur M. Schlesinger, Jr., *The Disuniting of America* (New York: Norton, 1992).

4. Gates's pluralist multicultural position has many points of contact with Finkielkraut's Enlightenment liberalism. The concept of "civic culture" is outlined in Henry Louis Gates, Jr., *Loose Canons: Notes on the Culture Wars* (New York: Oxford University Press, 1992), pp. xi–xix.

5. Finkielkraut's critique of the Reagan revolution was first published by the Team Foucault in the Italian newspaper *Corriere della Serra,* then published in Spanish as *La Nueva Derecha norteamericana (La Revancha y la Utopía)* (Barcelona: Editorial Anagrama, 1980). Habermas has similarly criticized neoconservatism in Germany and the United States, most recently in Jürgen Habermas, *The New Conservatism: Cultural Criticism and the Historians' Debate,* ed. and trans. by Shierry Weber Nicholsen; intro. by Richard Wolin (Cambridge, Mass: MIT Press, 1989).

6. For an account of Trilling, Bell and other members of this group, see Alan M. Wald, *The New York Intellectuals: The Rise and Decline of the anti-Stalinist Left from the 1930s to the 1980s* (Chapel Hill: University of North Carolina Press, 1987).

7. For an excellent collection of commentary and analysis of Bitburg as a political and cultural watershed, see Geoffrey Hartman, ed., *Bitburg*

in Moral and Political Perspective (Bloomington: Indiana University Press, 1986).

8. A helpful and critical summary of positions in the "Historikerstreit" is Richard J. Evans, *In Hitler's Shadow: West German Historians and the Attempt to Escape from the Nazi Past* (New York: Pantheon Books, 1989).

9. Walter Benjamin, "Theses on the Philosophy of History," in Hannah Arendt, ed., *Illuminations,* trans. Harry Zohn (New York: Schocken Books, 1966), pp. 254–55.

10. Alain Finkielkraut, *L'avenir d'une négation: Reflexion sur la question du génocide* (Paris: Editions du Seuil, 1982).

11. See Saul Friedlander, *When Memory Comes,* trans. Helen R. Lane (New York: Farrar, Straus, and Giroux, 1979); Saul Friedlander, ed., *Probing the Limits of Representation: Nazism and the Final Solution* (Cambridge, Mass.: Harvard University Press, 1992); Eric L. Santner, *Stranded Objects: Mourning, Memory, and Film in Postwar Germany* (Ithaca, N.Y.: Cornell University Press, 1990); Dominic LaCapra, "Representing the Holocaust: Reflections on the Historians' Debate," in Friedlander, ed., *Probing the Limits of Representation,* pp. 108–27; Yosef Yerushalmi, *Zakhor: Jewish Memory and Jewish History* (Seattle: University of Washington Press, 1982).

12. Alain Finkielkraut, "Conférence," speech delivered at the Prix Européen de l'Essai Charles Veillon (Bussigny, France: Fondation Charles Veillon, 1984).

13. Finkielkraut develops his position on democratic nationalism in Europe in his essay "Ne nous félicitons pas" ("Let's not congratulate ourselves"), in *Le Messager Européen,* no. 5, 1991, pp. 9–17.

14. Alice Y. Kaplan provides an excellent discussion of Finkielkraut as a postmodern thinker in her introduction to Finkielkraut's *Remembering in Vain.*

15. The centrality of Auschwitz in Adorno's thought is discussed by Shoshana Felman in Shoshana Felman and Dori Laub, *Testimony: Crises of Witnessing in Literature, Psychoanalysis, and History* (New York: Routledge, 1992), pp. 33–34. For Lanzmann's reflections on the Holocaust as a formative event for postwar culture, see "From the Holocaust to *Holocaust,*" *Telos,* no. 42, Winter 1979–1980, pp. 138–40 ff.; for Adorno's position, see "Elements of Anti-Semitism: Limits of Enlightenment," in Max Horkheimer and Théodor Adorno, *Dialectic of Enlightenment,* trans. John Cumming (New York: Continuum, 1986), pp. 168–208, and

Thédor Adorno, "Meditations on Metaphysics," in *Negative Dialectics,* trans. E. B. Ashton (New York: Continuum, 1973), pp. 362 ff.

CHAPTER ONE

1. Let me emphasize that I'm not attacking the book that Sartre devoted to the Jewish problem. This slight work remains a fascinating, fundamental, beneficial text. I'm only describing the romantic, projective manner I had of reading it – me, a Jew born four years after the war. If there is any criticism here, Sartre is certainly not the target.

CHAPTER TWO

1. Generations are born each day, at the will of styles or the journalistic desire to *make sense out of nothing.* Let's give this worn-out term the precise meaning that Jacques Juillard gave it: "A generation is composed of all the men and women who identify with a shared formative event or a common hardship that determines their outlook for the rest of their lives." So there is a May '68 generation, in the same way that, in France, there is a generation of the Algerian War, the Popular Front, and the Resistance (cf. *Le Nouvel Observateur,* Oct. 1979).

2. Milan Kundera, *Life is Elsewhere,* trans. Peter Kussi (New York: Viking Penguin, 1986), p.175.

3. This wasn't the case for our elders, our brothers during the Algerian revolt. They took sides for or against a war they were compelled to fight.

4. Pierre Goldman, *Dim Memories of a Polish Jew Born in France,* trans. Joan Pinkham (New York: Viking Press, 1977), p. 8.

5. The CRS is the Compagnie républicaine sécurité, the French state security police. Finkielkraut alludes to the '68 slogan that likened the French internal security service to the German ss of World War II. – TRANS.

6. Goldman, *Dim Memories,* p. 91.

7. See Jean-Paul Sartre, *Saint Genet, Actor and Martyr,* trans. Bernard Frechtman (New York: New American Library, 1963).

8. Which no doubt explains his silence during his first trial, this strange desire not to guarantee his own defense.

CHAPTER THREE

1. Chaïm Kaplan, *Scroll of Agony: The Warsaw Ghetto Diary of Chaïm Kaplan* (New York: Macmillan, 1965), p. 58.

2. David Bergelson. I discovered this passage in a very beautiful book

by Richard Marienstras, entitled *Etre un peuple en diaspora,* (Paris: Maspero, 1974).

3. Adolf Rudnicki, *Le Marchand de Lodz,* trans. Gilberte Crépy (Paris: Gallimard, 1969), p.62.

4. Jean-Claude Grumberg, *L'Atelier,* coll. "Théâtre ouvert" (Paris: Stock, 1979). "People told me, pay attention, Mr. Léon, but I said to myself, even if I get caught, what are they going to do? Give me another hole in the ass?"

5. A ratonnade was a punitive expedition or brutality carried out by Europeans against North Africans. – TRANS.

6. "Life in the Ghetto is stagnant and frozen. There are walls around us; we have no space, no freedom of action. Whatever we do we do illegally; legally we don't even have the right to exist." Chaïm Kaplan, *Scroll of Agony,* pp. 272–73. The important testimony of Emmanuel Ringelblum, *Notes from the Warsaw Ghetto: the Journal of Emmanuel Ringelblum,* trans. Jacob Sloan (New York: McGraw-Hill, 1958), is also required reading.

7. Indeed: pogroms *after* the concentration camps. On the predicament of Polish Jewry in the prewar years, see the work of Celia S. Heller, *On the Edge of Destruction: Jews of Poland between the Two World Wars* (New York: Columbia University Press, 1977). On the reality of Jewish isolation during the war, and its sources, see Lucy S. Dawidowicz, *The War Against the Jews* (New York: Holt, Rinehart, and Winston, 1975).

CHAPTER FOUR

1. On these initial difficulties, see Léon Poliakov, *From Voltaire to Wagner,* Vol. 3 of *The History of Anti-Semitism,* trans. Miriam Kochan (New York: Vanguard Press, 1965–), pp. 258–59. This historical analysis finds support in the fine novelistic testimony of Armand Lunel in his *Nicolo Peccavi*: "When the Revolution recognized their civil rights, our Jews, celebrating their enfranchisement, were nonetheless somewhat embarrassed. Many could break with the quasi-ritualistic isolation of the ghetto with only the greatest difficulty." (*Nicolo Peccavi ou l'Affaire Dreyfus à Carpentras* (Paris: Gallimard, 1976), p. 113) [trans. O'Neill and Suchoff].

2. See Michael Robert Marrus, *The Politics of Assimilation: A Study of the French Jewish Community at the Time of the Dreyfus Affair* (Oxford: Clarendon Press, 1971) pp. 58, 59, 76–77.

3. This opposition between the Jew and the Israelite goes back to the Middle Ages. It was used by the Church to anoint Christianity as the New Israel. In this appropriation of the name of their predecessors, it was im-

plied that God had called upon Christians to take over the role of the Chosen People. Two names, one glorious and one infamous, thus reconciled respect for a parent religion with contempt for its living practitioners. Isidore of Seville goes so far as to interpret the ancient separation of Israel and Judah as a prefiguration of the historic rupture between Christianity and Judaism. Cf. Salo Wittmayer Baron, *A Social and Religious History of the Jews,* Vol. 5 (New York: Columbia University Press, 1957) p. 126.

The Europe of the nineteenth century is humanist and no longer Christian: religion has lost its ideological monopoly; man, the heir or replacement of God, is the new principle of the universal. *Israelite* remains a noble word and *Jew* a pejorative name, but henceforth it's the people of Moses who are cut in half by this division. Regenerated, the Israelites deserve the fine name of man; as for the members of the synagogue who want to remain a separate nation, they exclude themselves from the human, and the name *Jew* is now reserved for these incurable holdovers.

4. Albert Londres, *The Jew has Come Home* (New York: R.R. Smith, 1931), p. 7.

5. See Marrus, *Politics of Assimilation,* p. 157.

6. See David H. Weinberg, *A Community of Trial: the Jews of Paris in the 1930s* (Chicago: University of Chicago Press, 1977) p. 50.

7. And what was the organization that, for every anti-Semite at the end of the nineteenth century, stood behind the Jewish conspiracy? The Alliance Israélite Universelle, the Society for Moral Progress (A. Chouraqui), founded in 1860 to assist Jews suffering persecution and to promulgate the idea of assimilation throughout the world.

8. In the Damascus Affair, Syrian Jews were tortured and killed in a case of blood libel (the charge that Christians were murdered so that their blood could be used to celebrate Passover). The Beilis trial in Russia resulted from similar charges brought against Menahem Mendel Beilis, which instigated a right-wing anti-Jewish campaign. Beilis was acquitted and settled in the United States; Bernard Malamud's novel *The Fixer* is based on his case.

9. Cited in Poliakov, *From Voltaire to Wagner,* p. 311. Edouard Drumont was a violently anti-Semitic journalist and anti-Dreyfusard who wrote *La France juive* (1886), an attack on Jews and Jewish financiers.

10. The passages in quotation marks are extracts from "On the Jewish Question," by Marx, in T. B. Bottomore, ed., *Karl Marx: Early Writings* (New York: McGraw-Hill, 1963), pp. 1–40. For a more detailed analysis

of this problem, see the appendix to this chapter, "Marx, Anti-Semitism and 'Class-Struggleism.' "

11. Cited in Georges Bernanos, *La Grande Peur des bien-pensants: Edouard Drumont* (Paris: B. Grasset, 1931), pp. 199–200.

12. Jules Guesde was a follower of Marx and a French socialist leader who designed the socialists' initial rejection of Dreyfus. On Guesde, French socialism and the Dreyfus case, see Robert L. Hoffman, *More than a Trial: The Struggle Over Captain Dreyfus* (New York: Free Press, 1980), p. 129. Jean Léon Jaurès founded and edited the socialist newspaper *L'Humanité.* He was assassinated just before the outbreak of World War I. See Zeev Sternhell, *Le Droit révolutionnaire: 1885–1914. Les Origines françaises du fascisme,* coll. *"Univers historique,"* (Paris: Editions du Seuil, 1978) p. 240.

13. See Vladimir Medem, *The Life and Soul of a Legendary Jewish Socialist: the Memoirs of Vladimir Medem,* trans. Samuel A. Portnoy (New York: Ktav Publishing House, 1979), pp. 268–69. The expression "class-struggleism" was introduced by Charles Péguy.

14. See Annie Kriegel, "Résistants communistes et Juifs persécutés," in Annie Kriegel, *Réflexion sur les questions juives* (Paris: Hachette, 1984), pp. 29–58. Even today, backers of Mr. Faurisson find support on the far Left. Certain revolutionary activists are more eager than the Nazis themselves to award the honor of being revisionist historians to sinister researchers pretending to demonstrate that the final solution never occurred. According to this logic, we'd have to consider the first ecstatic who treated France as if it were an island in the Indian Ocean as a revisionist geographer, and set up a televised debate between such advocates and mainstream geographers. But Spartacists of the old stripe keep faith with their heritage when they publish book after book contesting the existence of the gas chambers, while those nostalgic for the Reich have too much respect for Hitler to place the extermination of the Jews or the use of Ziklon B gas in doubt. Fascists know what they're looking for: only an obtuse Marxism would be able to place its faith in the lucubrations of revisionist pretense. In both strong and weak arguments based on class, Hitler was the docile instrument of Big Capital. There was no need to liquidate six million Jews; the horror was an abberation, and thus it never occurred. Why has legend of it spread? Just ask yourself who benefited from the crime, and you'll find the guilty party: Zionism of course, and its cousin, German imperialism, constantly working everyone up over the frightful extermination of the Jews, leaving them free to undertake worse

violence with impunity . . . Complete stupidity and absolute sloppiness. Here we see the apogee of "class struggleism": the moment when history is rewritten to fit a certain scheme, where one surgically operates on the past, like a nose job done to remove a disgrace from the face.

CHAPTER FIVE

1. Julien Benda, *La Jeunesse d'un clerc* (Paris: Gallimard, 1936) p. 29. Benda speaks here of his parents' generation (his father was born in 1827), but the analysis remains valid for the Jews of the first half of this century.

2. Franz Kafka, Letter to Max Brod, June 1921, in *The Basic Kafka,* intro. Erich Heller (New York: Washington Square Books, 1979), p. 292. This line from Kafka is the subject of a long commentary in the admirable book by Marthe Robert, *As Lonely as Franz Kafka* (New York: Harcourt, Brace, Jovanovich, 1982).

3. It persists and appears in the most unexpected areas. Anti-Semitism is much less easy to situate than thought in the good old days of the struggle against the Old World. It's our revolutionary naïveté that conflated the racist and the puritan, as if hatred of the other could be translated and completely diciphered in terms of sublimation. But prejudice is not the appanage of a moral majority or the frustrated. You find the same racist reflexes among the young who read *Actuel* as you do among authoritarian rednecks or in inhibited and dusty Old France. There is no lack of compatability between the relaxed style and the refusal of any and all difference. The racists of the eighties smoke joints, disdain old conventions and make love often. This is what we are slowly realizing.

CHAPTER SIX

1. Mathieu Dreyfus, *L'Affaire telle que je l'ai vécue* (Paris: B. Grasset, 1978), p. 46.

2. Portnoy, you'll remember, is the hero of Philip Roth's novel, *Portnoy's Complaint*. In the following pages, he will be the representative of all Jewish children who, within the confines of the family, have been taught simultaneously about Judaism, guilt and love.

CHAPTER SEVEN

1. In the same year – 1897 – the First Zionist World Congress and the Socialist Congress of Jewish Workers would take place, whence emerged the Bund, "United Jewish Workers of Lithuania, Russia and Poland."

Both sides claimed to offer a *specific* solution to the Jewish Question. But while the Zionists dreamed of reassembling the children of Israel in their biblical homeland, the Bundists violently rejected the idea of putting an end to the Diaspora. It was revolution not emigration they would preach, but a decentralized revolution joined by confederation, which would consolidate the ethnic uniqueness of different peoples instead of reducing it. At first hesitant and uncertain, the Bund's policy was strengthened through successive polemics with the Zionists and above all with the Bolsheviks, their implacable hereditary enemies. The Bundists, convinced socialists, pressed Lenin and his compatriots on the question of whether Jews had the right to a nation, even within a revolutionary regime. These heretical principles were enough to warrant the Bund's exclusion from the brand-new Soviet regime in 1921. A quite powerful force in Poland throughout the whole interwar period, the organization would be wiped out by Hitler's genocide.

2. Isaac Deutscher, *The Non-Jewish Jew and Other Essays* (New York: Oxford University Press, 1968), p. 112.

3. In France it was common to reduce prejudice to a kind of *folkloric xenophobia*. Jews responded to insults with a mixed response that today seems almost incomprehensible, with a combination of agressivity, indulgence and resignation. Listen to the testimony of Emmanuel Berl: "One day I was hounded all the way from the Carnot school to my home by cries of 'Down with the Jews.' I responded with my fists, and we exchanged blows. This is why we were so deceived by Hitler's version of anti-Semitism. Me, I was used to thinking of anti-Semitism as a reality, just the way it was, nothing really surprising, just like the dislike for Germans in France and the spite reserved by the North for the people of the beau, allons au cimetière (Paris: Gallimard, 1976) p. 16 [trans. O'Neill and Suchoff]. After the Dreyfus Affair and before Nazism, the myth of the "commercial confederacy marching arm in arm" appeared to be an indestructible figure of speech, but scarcely less innocent than the absent-minded professor, the flirtatious spouse or the mulish stubborness of the Breton: an inconsequential, unoriginal and almost excusable kind of racism among the wisdom of nations.

4. Bernard Lazare (1865–1903) was a French writer and one of Dreyfus' first and most ardent supporters in the Jewish community. See Léon Blum, *Souvenirs sur l'Affaire* (Paris: Gallimard, 1935) and Charles Péguy, *Notre Jeunesse* (Paris: Gallimard, 1933).

5. Bernard Lazare. On Lazare and Dreyfus, see Jean-Denis Bredin, *The Affair: The Case of Alfred Dreyfus,* trans. Jeffrey Mehlman (New York: George Brazilier, 1986), pp. 134–40.

6. Quoted in Weinberg, *A Community on Trial,* p. 135.

7. *Bougnoules* is a slang term for North Africans. – TRANS.

8. *Marranos* were Spanish or Portugese Jews who were forced to adopt Catholicism in 1492, but secretly practiced Judaism. – TRANS.

9. Franz Kafka, "An Introductory Talk on the Yiddish Language," delivered at the Jewish Town Hall in Prague, Feb. 18, 1912, trans. in Mark Anderson, ed., *Reading Kafka: Prague, Politics and the Fin de Siècle* (New York: Schocken Books, 1989), p. 264.

10. Lunel, *Niccolo Peccavi,* p. 75.

11. These citations are taken from Albert Cohen's novels *Mangeclous* (Paris: Gallimard, 1938), p. 260, and *Solal of the Solals* (London: G. P. Putnam's Sons, 1933) p. 112.

12. In Shmuel Trigano, *La Nouvelle Question juive* (Paris: Gallimard, 1979), "Ideas" Series, and in *Le Second Israel* (Paris: Les Temps Modernes, 1979), a special number of *Les Temps modernes* devoted to the Sephardic question, Trigano pushes this statification to its limit. In speaking of Ashkenazism and Sephardicism, he's clearly elevated this Israeli polarization into a metaphysical opposition on the order of Yin and Yang. This characteristic passage occurs shortly after the beginning of his piece: "History is thus the failed/emerging dialogue between masculine and feminine, of this world with the world to come, between the nations and Israel, between Ashkenazim and Sephardim." And further: "The Sephardim were the physical means in the period by which the destiny of Judaism and Israel were realized . . . for the Ashkenazim, except for the Hassidim, were dispersed throughout the West and remember Judaism through Yiddishkeit (and its cult) alone, through which they've sought to *diminish* the Jewish tradition" [trans. O'Neill and Suchoff].

13. Properly speaking, moreover, the Jewish Arabs are not Sephardic, as many of them have never had anything to do with Spain. But this amalgam seems to respond to two contradictory desires. The need for *respectability* first: as Haïm Vidal Sephiha suggests in the issue already cited of *Les Temps modernes,* certain North African Jews assume Spanish "letters of nobility" to rid their names of the Arab reference that is deemed pejorative. A desire to *politicize*: then the confrontation Ashkenazim/Sephardim is, in effect, the triumph of the political; a complex cultural reality is reduced to a simple and abrupt duel between dominant and dominated.

CHAPTER EIGHT

1. Introduction to *Zionism and Racism: Proceedings of the International Symposium. International Organization for the Elimination of All Forms of Racial Discrimination* (Tripoli: The Organization, 1976), p. 3. Several references will be made to this colloquium. By virtue of its varied contributors, including university scholars and politicians, from Western, Arab and Eastern countries, it provides a veritable compendium of anti-Semitic material.

2. Stefan Zweig, *The World of Yesterday: An Autobiography* (New York: Viking Press, 1943), p. 102.

3. Herzl, cited in Jean-Pierre Faye, *Migrations du récit sur le Peuple juif* (Paris: Belfond, 1974), p. 136.

4. Norman Cohn, *Warrant for Genocide: the Myth of the Jewish World-Conspiracy and the Protocols of the Elders of Zion* (New York: Harper and Row, 1969), p. 68.

5. *Zionism and Racism,* pp. 3–4.

6. This statement was made at UNESCO in 1976, by S. E. Abdallah Fadel, the Algerian Minister for Youth and Sports. See Jacques Givet, *The Anti-Zionist Complex,* trans. Evelyn Abel (Englewood, N.J.: SBS Publishers, 1982), p. 96.

7. An American delegation, charged with establishing an exhaustive documentary record of genocide against the Jews during World War II, visited Moscow in August 1979. Upon its arrival, the commentary of the news agency Tass evoked "the crimes of Zionists who worked hand in hand with Hitler's forces to exterminate the Jews during the Second World War" (*Le Monde,* Aug. 8, 1979). The imputation was hardly a new one: the young Soviet Republic had already accused Zionism of favoring the designs of British imperialism during the twenties and thirties, and during the thirties and forties those of Hitler. But it's only been recently, since the fifties, that anti-Zionism has achieved maximum profitability. There are no longer living Jews in the lexicon used to describe the Western democracies, there are only Zionists, and these rebaptized Jews, the politically accused with the new star of blue glued to their chests, have been condemned, among other atrocious crimes, of committing the massacre they themselves had to suffer. You can't stop progress.

8. Albert Memmi, *Jews and Arabs,* trans. Eleanor Levieux (Chicago: J. P. O'Hara, 1975) p. 75.

9. Norman Cohn, *Warrant for Genocide,* p. 263.

10. In addition to *Zionism and Racism* (already cited), see *Les Juifs et*

Israël vus par les théologiens arabes: extraits des procès verbaux de la 4e Confér-ence de l'Academie de recherches Islamiques Al Azhar, comp. and intro. D. F. Green, trans. Jean Christophe Palla (Geneva: Editions de l'Avenir,1972). What have these estimable theologians produced? They've put a sheen or a Koranic caution on political anti-Semitism born in the West.

11. See Yehoshafat Harkabi, *Arab Attitudes to Israel,* trans. Misha Louvish (Jerusalem: Israel University Press, 1972), p. 235.

12. Cited in Léon Poliakov, *De l'antisionisme à l'antisemitisme* (Paris: Plon, 1969), p. 148.

13. Cited in Givet, *Anti-Zionist Complex,* p. 111.

14. "Paras" are French military parachutists, some of whom rose up in a right-wing revolt against DeGaulle's policy during the Algerian War.

15. This quotation is taken from the novel by Herman Godsche, *Biar-ritz,* which is supposed to have served as the model for *The Protocols of the Elders of Zion.* See Cohn, *Warrant for Genocide,* pp. 38, 269.

16. Annie Kriegel, *Les Juifs et le monde moderne* (Paris: Editions du Seuil, 1977), p. 127.

17. See André Harris and Alain de Sédouy, *Juifs et Français* (Paris: B. Grasset, 1979), p. 194.

18. "Pain empoisonné et viande avariée," in *L'Arche,* Sept.–Oct. 1979.

CHAPTER NINE

1. Marienstras, *Etre un peuple en diaspora,* p. 134.

2. Bernard-Henri Lévy, "Discours au Memorial," in *Tel Quel,* no. 82, Winter 1979.

3. See *Les Nouvelles litteraires,* Sept. 13–19, 1979.

4. See "La vérité par hasard," conversation with Vladimir Jankélé-vitch, *Le Nouvel Observateur,* Jan. 14–20, 1980.

Index

Index

Quixote, Don, 24, 88

Rayman, Marcel, 27
Reagan, Ronald, 181
Reflections on the Jewish Question,
   xi, 10, 128
Resistance, French, 20, 26, 51;
   logic of class and denial of Jew-
   ish persecution by, 80
revolution, relation of Jews to,
   140
Robert, Marthe, 187
Rorty, Richard, viii
Rosenberg, Alfred, 152
Rosenzweig, Franz, xviii
Roth, Philip, vii, 187
Rouleau, Eric, 143
Rousseau, Jean Jacques, 61
Rudnicki, Adolph, 184 n.3
Russia, Czarist: Jews persecuted
   in, 66–67; Beilis affair and, 71;
   origin of *Protocols of the Elders of
   Zion* in, 160

Saint-Robert, Philippe de, 160
Santner, Eric, xiii, 182
Sartre, Jean-Paul, xi; *Reflections on
   the Jewish Question* considered,
   9–10, 19, 61, 128, 171, 183
Schlesinger, Arthur M., Jr., viii,
   181 n.3
Sédouy, Alain de, 191 n.17
Sephardic Jews, split with Ash-
   kenazi Jews, 141–44
Sephiha, Haim Vidal, 189 n.13
Shoah, xiii
Shylock, figure of, 66, 122
Six Day War, 128
Snake's Egg, The, 101
Stalin, Joseph, 20, 154–56
Sternhell, Zeev, 186 n.12
students, French: and leftist poli-
   tics, 9; and events and after-

math of May '68, 17–30, 94,
   134; and Pierre Goldman, 31–
   34; and socialism, 118

Talmud, 41
television: and politics, ix; and
   Jewish stereotypes, 40. *See also*
   Holocaust (television series)
Third World: and Jewish identity,
   134–35; replaces Jews in
   world's imagination, 135–36;
   forms of anti-Semitism in, 152
Torah, 41
Trenet, Charles, 19
Trigano, Shmuel, 169, 189 n.12
Trilling, Lionel, x
Trotsky, Leon, 20, 80

United Nations, resolution
   against Zionism, 129, 156

Villon, François, 29

Wagner, Richard, 49
Wald, Alan M., 181 n.6
Wannsee Conference, 44
War, modern, 86. *See also* Holo-
   caust
Warsaw, 26, 33, 37, 39; Ghetto
   uprising, 42, 50
Weinberg, David M., 185 n.6,
   189
Wolin, Richard, 181 n.5
Worker Stronghold, 167

xenophobia, 68

Yerushalmi, Yosef, xiii
Yiddish and Yiddishkeit: as
   unique culture, xiv, 36, 38, 41;
   culture distorted in Holocaust
   depictions, 42; loss of, 42, 113;
   despised by French Jews, 68;

200

Other volumes in the series Texts and Contexts: